THE PONY CLUB

The Worldwide Association of Young Riders

Patron: HRH The Princess Royal, KG KT GCVO QSO GCL
President: The Lady Lloyd Webber
Life Vice Presidents: Mary Anderson, Robin Danielli, Lt Col. Tadzik Kopanski
Chairman: Tim Vestey
Chief Executive: Marcus Capel

The Pony Club is an international voluntary youth organisation for those interested in horses, ponies and riding. It is the largest association of riders in the world. It is represented in no less than 27 countries and has a membership exceeding 110,000.

THE PONY CLUB HANDBOOK IS PUBLISHED BY THE PONY CLUB

Lowlands Equestrian Centre, Old Warwick Road, Warwick, CV35 7AX

Tel: 02476 698300
Email: enquiries@pcuk.org
Website: pcuk.org

Registered Charity No. **1050146**
Incorporated as a Company Limited by Guarantee
Registered in England No. **3072475**

Contents

PONY CLUB TEST
pcuk.org
FIRE SAFETY
pcuk.org
pcuk.org
ROAD RIDER
pcuk.org
FUNDRAISING
pcuk.org
CARE OF THE FOOT
pcuk.org
PONY CLUB TEST
C+
pcuk.org

Pony Club Committee Structure

Term of office ends at the end of year in brackets after each person's name.

TRUSTEES

Tim Vestey
(Chairman) (2026)
chairman@pcuk.org

Diane Pegrum
(Vice Chairman) (2026)

Andrew James
(2025)

Helen Jackson (A.R)
(2025)

Pleasance Jewitt
Chairman of A.R's (Ex Officio)

Anna Goodley
(2026)

Justine Baynes
(2026)

Nigel Howlett
(Treasurer) (2026)

MANAGEMENT COMMITTEE

Diane Pegrum (Chairman) (2026)

Nicky Morrison (A.R)

Abby Bernard (A.R)

Sarah MacDonald (Training)

Nigel Howlett (Treasurer)

Pleasance Jewitt (Area Representatives)

Lea Allen (Centre Membership)

Paul Darby (Safety and Welfare)

Patrick Campbell (Sports)

Clare Valori (Volunteers & Officials)

Andrew James (Rules & Compliance)

Marcus Capel (CEO)

Heidi Lockyer (Head of Charity)

Amy Veitch (Youth Advisory Council)

FINANCE & RISK COMMITTEE

Nigel Howlett
(Chairman and Treasurer) (2026)
treasurer@pcuk.org

Patrick Campbell (AR) (2024)
Finance Manager (Ex Officio)
Helen Jackson (A.R) (2024)
Isobel Mills (2025)
Andrew Tulloch (2025)
Tim Vestey (Trustee) (2026)

TRAINING COMMITTEE

Sarah MacDonald FBHS
(Chairman) (2024)
trainingchairman@pcuk.org

Carole Broad FBHS (2024)
Julie Campbell (2025)
Catherine Cawdron (2025)
Henry Church-Huxley (2025)
Vicki Macdonald (2025)
Michael Paveley (2025)
Paul Tapner (2025)
Hetta Wilkinson (A.R) (2025)
Will Harrison (2026)
Helen Jackson (A.R) (2026)
Janet Douglas (2025)
Ex-Officio Members:
Diane Pegrum (Vice Chairman)
Pleasance Jewitt (A.R Chairman)
Patrick Campbell (Chairman of Sports)
Lea Allen (Centre Membership Chairman)

CENTRE MEMBERSHIP COMMITTEE

Lea Allen (Chairman) (2025)
centrechairman@pcuk.org

Amelia Morris-Payne (2024)
Di Pegrum(Ex Officio)
Andrea Hurley (A.R) (2025)
Natalie O'Rourke MBE (2025)
Katy Powell (2025)
Hilary Wakefield (2025)
Michelle Macaulay (A.R) (2026)
Overseas Representative TBC

SAFETY AND WELFARE COMMITTEE

Paul Darby (Chairman) (2024)
safety@pcuk.org

Christine Gould (2024)
Ben Mayes (2024)
Hazel Warburton (2024)
Dr Ted Adams (2025)
Robin Bower (2025)
Stefanie Brazier (2025)
Sue Cheape (A.R) (2025)
Dr Michael Sinclair-Williams (2025)
Abby Bernard (A.R.) (2026)
Diane Pegrum (Ex Officio)

RULES AND COMPLIANCE COMMITTEE

Andrew James (Chairman) (2024)
rcchairman@pcuk.org

Karen Harris (A.R.) (2024)
Rosalind Slinger MBE (2024)
Christina Thompson (2024)
Abby Bernard (2025)
Ex-Officio Members:
Maureen Costello
Diane Pegrum
Hazel Warburton
Emma Holliwell - Operations Manager
Laura Armstrong - Lead Sports Officer

VOLUNTEERS AND OFFICIALS COMMITTEE

Clare Valori (Chairman) (2026)
volunteerschairman@pcuk.org

Maureen Costello (2024)
Helen Jackson (A.R) (2024)
Emma Neal (2024)
Catriona Willison (2024)
Hazel Warburton (2025)
Liz Lowry (2026)
Pleasance Jewitt (A.R) (2026)
Ex Officio Members
Diane Pegrum
Tim Vestey

CHAMPIONSHIP COMMITTEE 2024

Tim Vestey (Chairman) (2024)

Caroline Brown
Patrick Campbell
Paul Darby
Helen Jackson
Pleasance Jewitt
Diane Pegrum
Laura Armstrong
Marcus Capel
Beverley Laurie
Beryl Stringer

YOUTH ADVISORY COUNCIL

Amy Veitch (Chairman) (2026)
youthadvisory@pcuk.org

Charlotte Vickery
Myles Mentiply-Johnson
Faith Davey
Meg Cappaert
Beth Cole
Perdita Cottrill
Xanthe Goodman
Abigail Burbidge
Heliya Mohebi-Rad
Megan Hopkinson
Tatiane Mauree
Harleigh Oulton
Isobel Bean
Alicia Seagood-Pask

AREA REPRESENTATIVES

Pleasance Jewitt (Chairman) (2024)
area9@pcuk.org

AREA 1
Sue Cheape (2025)
area1@pcuk.org
07974 69535

AREA 2
Michelle Macaulay (2026)
area2@pcuk.org
07765 925850

AREA 3
Nicky Morrison (2024)
area3@pcuk.org
07850 617245

AREA 4
Robin Bower (2026)
area4@pcuk.org
07976 272272

AREA 5
Susan Goodridge (2026)
area5@pcuk.org
07765 327126

AREA 6
Patrick Campbell (2024)
area6@pcuk.org
07801 423898

AREA 7
Andrew James (2024)
area7@pcuk.org
01455 291273 / 07737 877697

AREA 8
Hetta Wilkinson (2024)
area8@pcuk.org
07880 728708 / 01206 330476

AREA 9
Pleasance Jewitt (2024)
area9@pcuk.org
01285 821715

AREA 10
Isobel Mills (2024)
area10@pcuk.org
07976 779140

AREA 11
Abby Bernard (2025)
area11@pcuk.org
07775 712512

AREA 12
Helen Jackson (2025)
area12@pcuk.org
01494 881321 / 07941 818738

AREA 13
Andrea Hurley (2025)
area13@pcuk.org
07967 683207

AREA 14
Louly Thornycroft (2024)
area14@pcuk.org
01258 860614

AREA 15
Deborah Custance-Baker (2025)
area15@pcuk.org
01392 861750 / 07889 260446

AREA 16
Karen Harris (2025)
area16@pcuk.org
01548 857617 / 07470 366000

AREA 17
Fran Rowlatt-McCormick (2026)
area17@pcuk.org
07912 627751

AREA 18
Julie Hodson (2024)
area18@pcuk.org
01239 654314

AREA 19
Anne Ekin (2024)
area19@pcuk.org
07711 630433

CENTRE COORDINATORS

Lea Allen (Chairman) (2025)
centrechairman@pcuk.org

AREA 1
Adrian Macleod
area1.centres@pcuk.org
07866 631875

AREA 2
Sarah Lewins
area2.centres@pcuk.org
07799 404246

AREA 3
John Gilbert
area3.centres@pcuk.org
07837 597561

AREA 4
John Gilbert
area4.centres@pcuk.org
07837 597561

AREA 5
John Gilbert
area5.centres@pcuk.org
07837 597561

AREA 6
Amelia Morris-Payne
area6.centres@pcuk.org
07816 955757

AREA 7
Amelia Morris-Payne
area7.centres@pcuk.org
07816 955757

AREA 8
Diane Pegrum
area8.centres@pcuk.org
07890 919558

AREA 9
Emma Stoba
area9.centres@pcuk.org
07792 839921

AREA 10
Emma Coates
area10.centres@pcuk.org
07973 677820

AREA 11
Sarah Glynn-Brooks
area11.centres@pcuk.org
07816 784487

AREA 12
Diane Pegrum
area12.centres@pcuk.org
07890 919558

AREA 13
Sally Blackmore
area13.centres@pcuk.org
07442 530080

AREA 14
Jacqui Bolt
area14.centres@pcuk.org
07790 970048

AREA 15
Jacqui Bolt
area15.centres@pcuk.org
07790 970048

AREA 16
Helen Moore
area16.centres@pcuk.org
07828 837784

AREA 17
Colleen Glasgow
area17.centres@pcuk.org
07885 800813

AREA 18
Emma Coates
area18.centres@pcuk.org
07973 677820

AREA 19
Sarah Lewins
area19.centres@pcuk.org
07799 404246

AREA 20 (Overseas)
TBC
overseas.centres@pcuk.org

SPORTS

DRESSAGE

Helen Griffiths
(Chairman) (2024)
dressagechairman@pcuk.org

Karen Burner (2024)
Cathy Burrell (2024)
Sue Coombe-Tennant (2024)
Rachael Coulter (2024)
Rory Howard (2024)
Isobel Mills (A.R) (2024)
Linda Pearce (2024)
Abby Bernard (A.R) (2025)

EVENTING

Patrick Campbell
(Chairman) (2025)
eventingchairman@pcuk.org

Catie Baird (2024)
Christina Thompson (2024)
Robin Bower (A.R) (2025)
Julie Campbell (2025)
Sue Cheape (A.R) (2025)
Harry Meade (2025)
Nicky Morrison (A.R) (2025)
Sarah Verney (2025)
Co-Opted Saskia Davies
Co-Opted Amy Veitch

ENDURANCE

Robert Blane
(Chairman) (2024)
endurancechairman@pcuk.org

Amanda Barton (2024)
Deborah Custance-Baker (A.R) (2024)
Tom Eaton-Evans (2024)
Fiona Williams (2024)
Rachael Chapple (2025)
Andrea Hurley (A.R) (2025)

HORSEMANSHIP

Amelia Morris-Payne
(Chairman) (2026)
horsemanshipchairman@pcuk.org

Elizabeth Hughes (2024)
Clare Valori (2024)
Lea Allen (2025)
Janet Douglas (2025)
Ruth Tarry (2026)
Fran Penn (2026)
Sue Cheape (A.R)(2026)
Andrew James (A.R)(2026)

MOUNTED GAMES

Ian Mariner
(Chairman) (2024)
mgchairman@pcuk.org

Alison Bell (2024)
Marcus Capel (2024)
Tracey Cooksley (2024)
Pennie Drummond (2024)
Marian Harding (2024)
Andrew James (A.R) (2024)
Catriona Willison (2024)
Vicky Dungait (2025)
Carol Howsam (2025)
Brian Ross (2025)
Fran Rowlatt-McCormick (A.R) (2026)

POLOCROSSE

Iain Heaton
(Chairman) (2025)
pxchairman@pcuk.org

Pam Drew (2024)
Hetta Wilkinson (A.R) (2024)
Angela Fynn (2025)
Jo Gale (2025)
Natalie Harpin (2025)
Lucinda Hayes(2025)
Laura Scott (2025)
Karen Harris (A.R) (2026)

POLO

Brig.Justin Stanhope-White
(Chairman) (2026)
polochairman@pcuk.org

Jenny Blake Thomas (2024)
Chris Eaton (2024)
Bethan Hitchman (2024)
Beverly Nicholls (2024)
Jo Whittington (2024)
Jilly Emerson (2025)
Pleasance Jewitt (A.R) (2025)
Louly Thornycroft (A.R) (2025)

PONY RACING

Steve Taylor
(Chairman) (2026)
racingchairman@pcuk.org

Jane Clark (2024)
Maureen Costello (2024)
Ruth Hurley (2024)
Nicky Morrison (A.R) (2024)
Louise Shepherd (2024)
Deborah Custance-Baker (A.R) (2025)
Sara Tremlett (2025)

SHOW JUMPING

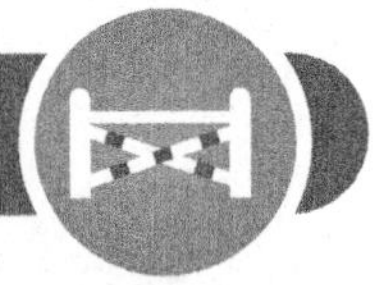

Hannah Jackson
(Chairman) (2025)
sjchairman@pcuk.org

Kirsty Hardstaff (2024)
Liz Lowry (2024)
Nicky Morrison (A.R) (2024)
Jane Ogle (2024)
Hetta Wilkinson (A.R) (2024)
Sue Peasley (2025)

TETRATHLON

Mandy Donaldson
(Chairman) (2026)
tetchairman@pcuk.org

Bee Bell (2024)
Jayne Bowman (2024)
Nick Cripps (2024)
Meg Green (2024)
Julie Hodson (A.R) (2024)
Rory Howard (2024)
Richard Mosley (Co-ordinator Representative) (2025)
Louly Thornycroft (A.R) (2024)
Liz Wilkinson (Co-ordinator Chairman) (2024)
Co-Opted Members
Alex Connors
Heather Greenslade
Judy Hardcastle
Zoe Kennerley

BRANCH OPERATIONS DIRECTORS

Maureen Costello (2024) – bod1@pcuk.org
Hazel Warburton (2024) – bod3@pcuk.org

For full details of The Pony Club Governance Structure visit pcuk.org

Rules of The Pony Club

(Text in bold type and sidelined denotes a change from the Rules as printed in the 2023 Handbook)

Any changes made to the Rules of The Pony Club during the year will be made available online at pcuk.org and Branches and Centres will be notified.

1. INTRODUCTION

Purpose

1.1 The Pony Club is a voluntary youth organisation for young people interested in ponies and riding. It is a Registered Charity and is subject to Charity legislation and to regulation by the Charity Commission. The Legal Objects of The Pony Club are set out in clause 4 of the Articles of Association (a copy of which may be obtained from The Pony Club Office upon payment of a fee).

The purpose of The Pony Club is:

- To promote and advance the education and understanding of the public and particularly children and young people, in all matters relating to horsemanship and the horse.
- To encourage the development of sportsmanship, unlocking potential by building resilience, confidence, teamwork and leadership skills.
- To support and develop the volunteering network to strengthen The Pony Club community and sustain life-long engagement with equestrianism.

1.2 The Pony Club Office is at Lowlands Equestrian Centre, Old Warwick Road, Warwick, CV35 7AX from where The Pony Club is managed by a permanent staff responsible to the governing body (the Trustees).

Health and Safety Policy

1.3 The Trustees are committed to ensuring, so far as is reasonably practicable, the Health and Safety of its employees, of everyone who assists The Pony Club in whatever capacity, Members and their families and members of the public who may be affected by the activities of The Pony Club.

1.4 The Trustees will ensure that management procedures and rules are in place to ensure that all Pony Club activities are run with due regard for the Health and Safety of all those people who may be affected by those activities and to ensure that all statutory duties are met.

1.5 Each employee, Area Representative, and District Commissioner/Centre Proprietor shall be given such information, instruction and training as is necessary for them to perform their duties in safety. When tasks require particular skills additional to those of The Pony Club staff and volunteers, a competent person or contractor with the necessary experience and training shall be engaged.

1.6 Each employee and volunteer will be expected to co-operate with The Pony Club or District Commissioner/Centre Proprietor to ensure that all statutory duties are complied with and to ensure that all work activities are carried out safely. Each individual has a legal obligation to take reasonable care for his or her own Health and Safety, and for the safety of others who may be affected by his or her acts or omissions. Any person who is concerned about any issue relating to Health and Safety should raise the matter with their District Commissioner/Centre Proprietor or manager at the earliest available opportunity.

Organisational Arrangements

1.7 The Chief Executive and the Pony Club Office shall on behalf of the Trustees

i. Ensure that Rules and procedures are published and updated regularly to cover all Pony Club activities;
ii. Ensure that adequate Employer's Liability and Public Liability insurance cover, as determined by The Trustees of The Pony Club, is obtained;
iii. Ensure that adequate training and instruction is provided for Area Representatives, District Commissioners, Volunteers and Employees;
iv. Maintain a central record of competent Coaches and their attendance at professional development training. Coaches may be deemed to be competent by virtue of qualification, achievement or experience in one or more fields relevant to Pony Club activities;
v. Ensure that all activities organised by The Pony Club are run with due regard to the Health and Safety of everyone who may be affected by that activity;
vi. Ensure that adequate safeguarding procedures are notified to Area Representatives, District Commissioners and Centre Proprietors for implementation at all Pony Club activities;
vii. Maintain effective communications on Health and Safety issues with employees, Area Representatives, District Commissioners and Centre Proprietors;
viii. Require accidents to be investigated to identify the causes so that actions may be taken to reduce the possibility of a recurrence.

1.8 District Commissioners shall operate their Branches in accordance with the Rules of The Pony Club and statutory requirements and with due regard for the health and safety of their Members, parents and guardians, volunteers and any other person who may be affected by the activities organised by the Branch.

1.9 Area Representatives are responsible for monitoring the Health and Safety performance of the Branches in their Area.

1.10 Pony Club Linked Riding Centres are responsible for their own Health and Safety arrangements. These will be monitored by their Area Centre Coordinator and reported to The Pony Club Office as part of the Centre annual visit.

Responsibilities of Employees, Officials, Volunteers, Coaches and Contractors

1.11 All persons acting on behalf of The Pony Club or carrying out work for The Pony Club must -

i. Take reasonable care for their own Health and Safety;
ii. Consider the safety of other persons who may be affected by their acts or omissions;
iii. Work within the limits of their own training and competence and the information and instructions they have received;
iv. Refrain from intentionally misusing or recklessly interfering with any equipment provided for Health and Safety reasons;
v. Report any hazardous defects in plant and equipment or shortcomings in the existing safety arrangements to a member of the Branch Committee, or their immediate Pony Club contact, as soon as practicable;
vi. Report all accidents to a member of the Branch Committee, or their immediate Pony Club contact.

1.12 Health and Safety is to be given priority

over any other Pony Club activity.

Other Legislation

1.13 It is also the policy of The Pony Club to take account of, and to implement as required, legislation on human rights, legislation which impacts voluntary youth organisations, and which regulates the care and supervision of young people.

1.14 In relation to equity, equality and diversity, The Pony Club

i. aims to ensure that all people, irrespective of race, gender, ability, ethnic origin, social status or sexual orientation have equal opportunities to take part in equestrianism at all levels and in any roles;
ii. seeks to educate and guide Pony Club Members, their employees and volunteers on the ownership, adoption and implementation of its Equity, Equality and Diversity Action Plan;
iii. intends to raise awareness of equity, equality and diversity through the implementation of this policy and the adoption of the Equity, Equality and Diversity Action Plan; and, as a result of this process
iv. aims to monitor, review and evaluate progress in achieving the stated aims and objectives and to feed back to member bodies on progress made.

1.15 The Pony Club will ensure that its recruitment and selection procedures are fair, transparent and meet the appropriate legal requirements.

2. DEFINITIONS

2.1 In these Rules:

"Area" means a geographic sub-division of Great Britain and Northern Ireland.

"Area Centre Coordinator" means the person responsible for supporting Centres within an Area and for advising on Centre Membership issues within that Area.

"Area Representative" means the person responsible for overseeing Pony Club activities within an Area.

"BETA" means the British Equestrian Trade Association.

"BEF" means the British Equestrian.

"Branch" means an operating sub-division of The Pony Club, organising Pony Club activities at a local level.

"Branch Member" means a Member of a Branch.

"Branch Operations Director" means a person appointed by the Management Committee to assist relationships and communication, when required, between Branches and Area Representatives, and the Pony Club Office, and also to mediate in inter-Branch or intra-Branch disputes. He will be appointed for 3 years but may offer himself for re-appointment.

"Centre Member" includes both a Centre Member and a Centre Plus Member unless the context otherwise requires and means someone who is a Member through a Pony Club Centre.

"Centre Membership Scheme" means the approval of riding establishments as a Pony Club Linked Riding Centre administered by The Pony Club Office for the membership of Centre Members.

"Centre Plus Member" means someone who is a Member through a Pony Club Linked Riding Centre who has regular access to ride a horse/pony outside of Centre organised activities. This includes someone who owns, leases or borrows a horse/pony.

"Championships" means The Pony Club

Championships. including where the context requires the Pony Club Tetrathlon, Polo and Endurance Championships and the Regional Championships.

"Charity" means "The Pony Club" as constituted as a Registered Charity.

"Children of the Family" includes siblings, half siblings, adopted children, foster children, and children who have a guardian residing at their address.

"Company Member" means a person who is entitled to vote at general meetings of The Pony Club being the Trustees, the Area Representatives, the Branch Operations Directors and the Chairmen of all National Committees.

"Designated Funds" are funds that have been earmarked by the Trustees or by a Branch Committee for specific projects.

"District Commissioner" means the person responsible for administering Pony Club activities within a Branch.

"Equestrian Professional" means a person who is financially interested in letting out or selling horses, in instructing in equitation or keeping liveries or other equestrian facilities.

"Family Membership" means membership available for up to a maximum of 5 Children of the Family living at the same permanent address who are Members of the same Branch.

"Free reserves" are the assets of the Branch (excluding fixed assets) less its liabilities and less any Restricted or Designated Funds.

"Handbook" means the annual publication giving information about The Pony Club.

"he" means either he or she and "his" means either his or her.

"Health and Safety Policy" means the Policy as stated in the introduction to these Rules.

"Management Committee" means the executive body responsible for the day-to-day operation of The Pony Club, whose membership is defined in Rule 4.10.

"Member" includes a Branch Member and a Centre Member unless the context otherwise requires.

"Membership Subscription Year" means the period of twelve months commencing on the date the Member's subscription is paid and terminating on the day before the anniversary of this date.

"Non-Riding Member" means a Branch Member who is eligible to take part only in unmounted Pony Club activities (e.g. Horse and Pony Care, Quiz, Triathlon and unmounted rallies).

"Parents" shall include individuals with parental responsibility.

"Pony" means either a pony or a horse, except where the terminology is clearly specific to a pony.

"Pony Club Centre" or "Centre" means a Riding Centre that has been accepted to participate in the Centre Membership Scheme as a Pony Club Linked Riding Centre.

"Pony Club Office" or "The Office" means the central office maintained by The Pony Club, which is also the registered address of The Pony Club.

"Pony Club Year" means the period from 1 January to the following 31 December.

"Restricted Funds" are monies that have been given by a donor with conditions on how they are to be spent.

"Riding Member" means a Branch Member

who is eligible to take part in all Pony Club activities whether mounted or unmounted.

"Rules" and "Rules of The Pony Club" mean the Rules of The Pony Club, as published in the Handbook, and displayed on the website. The Rules are determined by the Trustees (in the spirit and best interests of The Pony Club and its objectives). The Rules may be added to, cancelled in whole or in part or altered, as the Trustees or the Company Members at a general meeting deem necessary. The Trustees may also make temporary rules for a limited period. Changes or additions to the Rules will be published on the website. Any query about the operation of the Rules or request for clarification should be referred to the Trustees.

"Safey and Welfare Committee" means the Committee established to perform the functions of the Health and Safety and Safeguarding Committee established under the Articles of Association.

"Website" means the website of The Pony Club, available at pcuk.org.

2.2 For the purposes of these Rules and individual sports rule books, a horse or pony shall be deemed to reach the age of 1 on the 1st January following the date on which it is foaled and shall be deemed to become a year older on each successive 1st January.

3. PERIOD OF OFFICE

3.1 The Chairman, Vice-Chairman and Treasurer shall serve in that capacity for a maximum of two terms of 3 years. No Trustee may serve for more than three consecutive terms of three years. They may then stand again after a period of 3 years has elapsed, up to a maximum of a further three consecutive terms of three years.

3.2 In exceptional circumstances, the Trustees may agree to an extension for a person who otherwise would have to retire, but for a maximum of 1 year.

3.3 This Rule shall prevail if it is in conflict with any other Rule.

4. STRUCTURE

The Trustees

4.1 The Trustees are the ultimate authority of The Pony Club (subject to review by the Company Members at the Annual General Meeting) and are responsible for the general administration and management of the affairs of The Pony Club. The Trustees may delegate their authority to subsidiary bodies, officials and employees. A register shall be maintained of all delegations and authority limits.

4.2 Reporting to the Trustees will be the Management Committee, the Finance and Risk Committee, the **Safety and Welfare Committee** and the Chief Executive.

Chairman of The Pony Club

4.3 The Chairman of The Pony Club will be nominated by the Trustees after consultation with the Volunteers and Officials Committee. The Trustees' nomination will then be subject to confirmation by the Company Members at the Annual General Meeting. The Chairman will hold office for three years from 1st January after his appointment and, subject to Rule 3, a retiring Chairman will be eligible for re-appointment. **The Chairman may attend all meetings of any Committee of which he is not a member and have the right to speak at each such meeting but shall not have a vote.**

Vice Chairman of The Pony Club

4.4 The Trustees will nominate a Vice Chairman of The Pony Club after consultation with the Volunteers and Officials Committee, to assist the Chairman

in the performance of his duties. The Trustees' nomination will then be subject to confirmation by the Company Members at the Annual General Meeting. The Vice Chairman will hold office for three years from 1st January after his appointment and, subject to Rule 3, a retiring Vice Chairman will be eligible for re- appointment.

4.5 If the person appointed as Chairman or Vice Chairman is an Area Representative or Sports Chairman, he will resign his original position.

Honorary Appointments

4.6 The Trustees may make honorary appointments, such as President, or Vice President. The holders of such appointments will not, by virtue solely of that office, be members of any Pony Club Committee.

Finance and Risk Committee

4.7 The Finance and Risk Committee will monitor the integrity of The Pony Club's financial statements and internal controls. It will also review the budgets, the statutory accounts and the risk management systems, and will report on these to the Trustees at each meeting (so far as applicable). The Committee will also make recommendations to the Trustees in relation to the appointment and remuneration of the auditors and will have as specific terms of reference to

- oversee the financial reporting and disclosure process.
- monitor the choice of accounting policies and principles.
- oversee the hiring and performance and independence of the external auditors
- monitor internal controls and compliance with laws and regulations
- oversee preparation of the Trustees' annual report
- monitor the collation and updating of the risk register
- oversee the implementation of best anti-fraud practices
- oversee the implementation of appropriate whistle blowing practices
- implement and manage an appropriate board review process

4.8 The Committee will meet separately with the external auditors to discuss matters that the committee or auditors believe should be discussed privately and will be chaired by the Treasurer and shall include the Treasurer, another Trustee, two members nominated by the Area Representatives, and such other persons of appropriate expertise as may be nominated by the Trustees. The Committee will meet as required, but at least twice each year, and the **Finance Manager** (or other member of staff nominated by the Chief Executive) shall attend each meeting.

Management Committee

4.9 The Management Committee is the executive body charged with the management of The Pony Club in accordance with the policies and guidelines established by the Trustees and for the avoidance of doubt will be responsible for determining any matters which do not fall to be determined by any other committee.

4.10 The Vice Chairman of The Pony Club will chair the Management Committee and its membership will be:

- The Vice Chairman
- The Chairman of the Training Committee
- The Chairman of the Safety and Welfare Committee
- The Chairman of the Centre Membership Committee
- The Chairman of the Area Representatives' Committee
- The Chairman of the Chairmen of the Sports Committee
- The Chairman of the Rules and

Compliance Committee
- The Chairman of the Finance and Risk Committee
- The Chairman of the Volunteers and Officials Committee
- **The Chairman of the Youth Advisory Council.**
- Two members elected by the Area Representatives
- The Chief Executive Officer
- The Head of Charity

4.11 Other members of the staff of The Pony Club may attend the meetings at the invitation of the Chairman of the Management Committee.

4.12 The elected Area Representatives on the Management Committee will serve for a period of three years. When required, an election for a new Area Representative member of the Management Committee will be held at the last meeting in the year of the Area Representatives' Committee, with the appointment to be effective from the following 1st January. Each member of the Management Committee shall have a nominated substitute who shall be entitled in the absence of that member to attend the Management Committee in his stead.

4.13 It will not normally be appropriate for a member of the Management Committee who is not a member of staff to hold the same position for more than three consecutive terms of three years but he may stand again after a period of one year has elapsed to a maximum of a further three consecutive terms of three years.

4.14 An Area Representative **(other than the Chairman of the Area Representatives' Committee**) serving as an elected Area Representative Trustee may not simultaneously serve on the Management Committee.

4.15 The Chairman of the Chairmen of Sports Committee will serve for a period of three years and may not immediately stand for reelection.

4.16 The Management Committee will meet at regular intervals.

4.17 Management Committee decisions will normally be made by open vote. However, the Management Committee may decide to have a secret ballot if a majority of those present so wish. All members will have equality of voting on all matters. The Chairman of the Management Committee will have a second or the casting vote in the event of equality of votes. A quorum will consist of not fewer than five members of the Management Committee entitled to vote.

Rules applicable to all committees

4.18 Unless specifically provided for elsewhere in these rules, the following Rules shall apply to all committees, with the exception of the Appeals Committee: -

4.19 Each committee shall have a Chairman, who will normally hold office for three years, terminating at the end of the third Pony Club Year, although he may offer himself for re-appointment.

4.20 Nominations for the Chairman can be made by the relevant Committee members and by Company Members. If there is one nominee, he will be appointed Chairman for a three year term. If more than one nomination is received, a vote by committee members and Company Members will determine who is appointed.

4.21 If the Chairman of any committee loses the confidence of his committee members, and he is unwilling to resign, then this should be reported to the Management Committee in writing, signed by a majority of the committee members.

The Management Committee will appoint a person to investigate fully and, if necessary, report back on the facts. The Management Committee, in its absolute discretion, may end the appointment of a committee chairman or any other committee member at any time upon giving written notice to the individual. The Management Committee will normally seek representations from the individual concerned and will normally give reasons for its decision.

4.22 Persons appointed to committees established under these rules are expected to contribute fully to the working of that committee and therefore any persons who, without reasonable excuse, fails to attend (either in person or by conference call) three consecutive meetings of the committee shall cease to be a member of that committee.

4.23 Each committee shall include two Area Representatives. Every Area Representative shall be offered a place on at least one committee. Area Representatives will serve on a committee for three Pony Club Years.

4.24 No later than 1st August each year, each Area Representative shall be invited to indicate the committees on which he wishes to serve. These should be given in order of preference. The Management Committee shall then allocate the Area Representatives to committees.

4.25 Other than the Area Representatives, persons will be invited to become members of committees because of their expertise in a particular area. They will serve for a period of three years but may offer themselves for reelection. All vacancies must be advertised on The Pony Club website. All candidates must be nominated in writing by a Company Member. If there are more nominations than there are places available, then a vote will be held. Those entitled to vote will be the existing members of the Committee, both continuing and retiring, and the Company members.

4.26 A list of the proposed composition of each committee for the coming year shall be submitted to the Annual General Meeting for ratification.

4.27 Proposals to fill vacancies that exist or occur after the list of the proposed composition of each committee for the coming year has been ratified by the Annual General Meeting, shall be submitted to the next Management Committee meeting after the vacancy arises for approval.

4.28 All members of a committee shall have equal voting rights, except that co-opted advisors shall not have a vote. The chairman of the committee shall have **a second or** the casting vote in the event of equality of votes. Any three members of a committee will form a quorum.

4.29 Subject to rules 4.30 below, each Committee shall comprise of a maximum membership as shown in the table below. Committees are free to operate with fewer members than the upper limit.

Committee	Upper Limit
Centre Membership	10
Finance & Risk	10
Management	14
Rules and Compliance	10+5 Ex Officio
Training	10+4 Ex Officio
Trustees	12
Volunteers and Officials	10
Safety and Welfare Committee	10
Youth Advisory Council	16
Dressage	10

Endurance	10
Eventing	10
Horsemanship	10
Mounted Games	12
Polo	10
Polocrosse	10
Pony Racing	10
Show Jumping	10
Tetrathlon	10+2 Ex Officio

4.30 If a Committee wishes to exceed the maximum membership shown in the table in rule 4.29, it may apply to the Management Committee for permission to do so. If the Management Committee is satisfied that exceptional circumstances exist justifying such an increase it may approve the request. The approval of the Management Committee may be given subject to such conditions as the Management Committee sees fit and may be time limited. If at any time a committee exceeds the maximum membership shown in the table in rule 4.29 (excluding those who are ex officio members of the Committee, no new members may be appointed to the Committee until retirements lead to member numbers dropping below the upper limit.

4.31 With the agreement of his Committee, a Committee Chairman may co-opt advisors on to the Committee. Co-option should be to provide a specific service or specialist advice. Co-opted advisors will attend committee meetings only until 31st December in the year they are co-opted. They may be co-opted again but only with the renewed agreement of the committee. Co-opted committee advisors do not have voting rights.

Area Representatives' Committee

4.32 The Area Representatives' Committee will comprise the 19 Area Representatives and will be chaired by an elected Area Representative. The Area Representative elected as the Chaiman of the Area Representatives' Committee will serve as one of the two Area Representatives elected as a Trustee under Article 22.4 of the Articles of Association of The Pony Club.

Those persons who will be Area Representatives in the year following the vote are eligible to propose, second or vote for Chairman of the Area Representatives Committee. i.e. retiring Area Representatives are not eligible. The Committee will meet at least twice a year. The Branch Operations Directors shall be entitled to attend meetings of the committee but shall not have a vote.

Appeals Committee

4.33 In the event that any matter cannot be resolved by the Area Representatives, the Area Centre Coordinators, the Branch Operations Directors, the Management Committee, the Centre Membership Committee or the relevant Sport Committee, the Chairman of the Management Committee will establish a committee of three or more Company Members, retired Area Representatives or retired Chairmen of a Sports Committee at least one of whom must be an Area Representative. The committee will choose one of their number to act as chairman. The members chosen must not have a conflict of interest.

4.34 The Chairman will have a second or the casting vote in the event of equality of votes.

4.35 The decisions of the Appeals Committee shall be final.

4.36 Any three members of the Appeals

Committee will form a quorum.

Sport Committees

4.37 There shall be formed a committee for each sport and activity listed in rule 4.29 comprising two Area Representatives plus other persons with relevant knowledge and experience of each sport or activity.

Subject to the overall control of the Management Committee, these Committees will in each case have responsibility for the administration of their sport/activity within The Pony Club.

Each Committee will maintain a sport/activity Rule Book which is published annually, and they adjudicate on any matters requiring resolution within their sport. These sport/activity Rule Books form part of the Rules of The Pony Club. Each Committee shall meet as and when necessary to perform their functions.

4.38 With the approval of the Management Committee, a newly appointed or re-appointed Sport Chairman may require up to 50% of the Sport Committee to resign.

Chairmen of Sports Committee

4.39 The Chairmen of Sports Committee will comprise the Chairmen of each of the **Committees created under Rule 4.37.** The Committee will elect a Chairman from amongst its number who will hold office for three years and will represent the Committee on the Management Committee in accordance with rules 4.10 and 4.15. The Committee will act as a forum for discussion of issues affecting the various sports. It will as far as reasonably practicable endeavour to ensure that there is consistency between the organisation and rules of the various sports whilst recognising that there will be areas in which they differ.

Training Committee

4.40 The Training Committee has responsibility for advising the Management Committee on:

- The training of Pony Club coaches;
- The training of Pony Club Members;
- All elements of horsemanship and horsemastership within competitions;
- The commissioning of coaching and training publications;
- All aspects of the A, AH, B+ and B Tests including the administration of tests;
- The appointments and removal of assessors to and from the Panel of Assessors for 'A' and 'AH' Tests.

4.41 The Training Committee shall meet annually to recommend any changes required to the syllabus of each Test, or to the fees charged for 'B' test and above.

Centre Membership Committee

4.42 The Centre Membership Committee has responsibility for advising the Management Committee on:

- The administration of the Centre Membership Scheme and all matters affecting the interests of Centre Members
- The criteria to be met and the standards required of Pony Club Centres to join the Centre Membership Scheme

4.43 To assist the Centre Membership Committee in the exercise of its functions an Area Centre Coordinator will be appointed for each Area.

Safety and Welfare Committee

4.44 The Safety and Welfare Committee will meet as required and will have responsibility for reviewing and advising the Trustees on:

- The Health and Safety Policy of The Pony Club
- The Pony Club Safeguarding Policy
- All matters concerning compliance with

the safer recruitment requirements including disclosure checks and safeguarding training.

Rules and Compliance Committee

4.45 The Committee will be responsible for maintaining the Rules of The Pony Club and recommending changes to the Trustees as they may be required. The Committee will scrutinise the various rule books to ensure consistency and set codes of conduct and standards to apply throughout The Pony Club. All complaints and disputes will be dealt with by the Committee.

4.46 The Branch Operations Directors will be members of the Committee. Two Area Representatives will also be members and the Committee will have power to co-opt additional members from time to time. It is recommended that one member of the Committee should have legal experience.

Volunteers and Officials Committee

4.47 The Committee will oversee the recruitment of volunteers to The Pony Club and for advising on the processes by which they are elected. The Committee will also approve and/or ratify new District Commissioners.

4.48 The Committee will ensure that suitable training and development is provided for volunteers and that they are duly rewarded and recognised. The Committee will consult with volunteers as it sees fit.

4.49 Membership of the Committee must include at least two Trustees and two Area Representatives. The Chairman of The Pony Club shall be ex officio a member of the Committee and may attend at his discretion.

Pony Club Youth Advisory Council

4.50 There shall be established a body to be known as the Youth Advisory Council ("the YAC") comprised solely of Pony Club Members which shall have the following responsibilities:

- **to be a representative group of current Pony Club Members with varied experiences of the organisation, including membership type, geographic location and lived experience.**
- **to advise the Management Committee and to work closely with Pony Club Staff to amplify the youth voice on matters affecting the interests of Pony Club Members**
- **to ensure The Pony Club is a welcoming, inclusive organisation for young people to join, by providing advice and recommendations on developments within the organisation.**

4.51 Membership of the YAC is open to Pony Club Members aged between 14 and 25 who must be Pony Club Members at the time of their application to join the YAC and who maintain their membership during their term on the YAC. Any member of the YAC whose membership of The Pony Club lapses for a period of more than one month will cease to be a member of the YAC.

4.52 Members will be appointed to the YAC for a three-year term. The maximum number of members of the YAC will be sixteen. It will meet online six times each year with support from Pony Club Staff. The Chairman and Vice Chairman of The Pony Club shall be entitled to attend these meetings.

4.53 The Trustees will make rules specifying the criteria candidates must meet to be appointed to the YAC as well as the process to be followed for their appointment.

A Panel of senior volunteers and staff appointed by the Trustees and led by the Head of Charity will meet to consider applications from individuals wishing to be appointed as members of the YAC.

4.54 The members of the YAC will elect from within their number, a Chairman and Vice Chairman. The Chairman of the YAC will be a member of the Management Committee.

4.55 A Sub-committee of the Trustees consisting of the Chairman, the Vice Chairman and the Chief Executive will meet annually to appoint two members of the YAC to represent The Pony Club on the Pony Club International Alliance Youth Advisory Committee. The role of the two members appointed will be to:

- **Collaborate with other members of the Pony Club International Alliance to further PCIA benefits to our members.**
- **Communicate Pony Club International Alliance initiatives to Pony Club YAC and the wider PCUK community.**
- **Contribute to Pony Club International Alliance initiatives and actively promote the initiatives out in the field.**
- **Represent the membership at international level.**

Treasurer of The Pony Club

4.56 The Treasurer of the Pony Club shall be appointed by the Trustees and will hold office for a period of three years. Subject to Rule 3, a retiring Treasurer will be eligible for re-appointment for a further term of 3 years. The Treasurer, with the support of the **Finance Manager** will be responsible for all financial matters affecting The Pony Club.

4.57 Not later than the end of October each year, the Treasurer of The Pony Club will submit to the Management Committee a draft budget for the following Pony Club Year, together with recommendations on annual subscriptions and capitation fees for that year. The Management Committee will then forward to the Trustees its recommendations as to the budget for the following Pony Club Year for approval (with or without modifications) by the Trustees.

4.58 At each Meeting of the Trustees, the Treasurer and/or the **Finance Manager** will give a financial report, during which they will comment on any material variations from the approved budget.

Chief Executive

4.59 The Chief Executive will be an employee of The Pony Club, responsible for administering the activities of The Pony Club and the Office within the policies and procedures established by the Trustees and in accordance with statutory requirements and the approved budget. He will report to the Chairman of The Pony Club and, through him, to the Trustees. **He will attend all meetings of the Trustees, and all general meetings and such committee meetings as he may choose. He will have the right to speak at each such meeting but shall not have a vote, except on the Management Committee. He will, together with the Chairman or Vice Chairman (or their nominee), represent The Pony Club at meetings of the Pony Club International Alliance.**

4.60 The Chief Executive may appoint or dismiss staff (other than members of the Senior Management Team) with the agreement of the Chairman of The Pony Club.

4.61 In the event of a vacancy for the position of Chief Executive or any other member of the Senior Management Team, the Trustees will establish a Recruitment sub-committee to recruit a new Chief Executive or member of the Senior Management Team as the case may be. This sub-committee will consist of no more than six members, to include the Chairman of The Pony Club (who will act as Chairman of the sub-committee) and the Treasurer of The Pony Club. The other members of the sub-committee will be drawn from the Trustees. The sub-committee will decide upon the selection policy and methods and will have absolute and irrevocable authority, on behalf of The Pony Club, to make an offer of employment to the candidate that it chooses. In the event of equality of votes, the Chairman of The Pony Club will have a second or the casting vote.

The Handbook

4.62 The Pony Club Handbook will be published annually. It will include these Rules (but not the Sport Rules); annual subscriptions and test fees; names of the Trustees, the committees established under this Rule 4, Branch officials, Area Centre Coordinators and Centre Proprietors; details of Insurance cover and information on Pony Club merchandise. The Handbook may be published in electronic form.

Bankruptcy

4.63 Any Trustee, Company Member or District Commissioner, who becomes bankrupt or makes a composition with his creditors, shall be disqualified from office and his appointment shall be terminated immediately. No person who is an undischarged bankrupt may be appointed to any of these offices. This Rule shall also apply to any officer or member of a Branch Committee who has any responsibility for the financial affairs of the Branch.

5. CONFLICT OF INTEREST

5.1 At all levels of The Pony Club, from the Trustees to Branch Sub-Committees, avoidance of any potential conflict of interest must be strictly observed. Whenever an individual has a personal interest in a matter to be discussed at a meeting of a committee of which he is a member, he must: -

a. Declare his interest before discussion begins.
b. Be absent from the meeting for that item, unless expressly invited to remain to provide information.
c. Not be counted in the quorum for that part of the meeting.
d. Be absent during the vote and have no vote on the matter.

5.2 Normally, a person who is an Equestrian Professional will not be eligible for appointment as an Area Representative or as a member of any committee or sub-committee established under these Rules (except for membership of the Centre Membership Committee or the Training Committee). The Management Committee however, at its discretion, may decide to approve the appointment of an Equestrian Professional as an Area Representative and may attach to the approval such conditions as the Management Committee in its absolute discretion considers appropriate. In such a case, the person must submit a written declaration that he has read and understood the Conflict of Interest Policy of The Pony Club, as defined in this Rule, and that he will adhere to it. Equestrian Professionals who are members of any committee (including the Centre Membership Committee and the Training Committee) or the Management Committee must also submit such a declaration. This Rule shall not be applied retrospectively.

5.3 A person empowered to take decisions on behalf of The Pony Club must ensure that those decisions are made in the best interests of The Pony Club.

6. MINUTES

6.1 All meetings of the Trustees, the Finance and Risk Committee, the Management Committee, the **Safety and Welfare** Committee and the committees established under these Rules must be minuted and, subject to rule 6.2, copies of the minutes will be distributed to all members of these bodies, whether they were present at the meeting or not. Copies of the minutes will also be distributed as follows: -

- The Finance and Risk Committee – to the Trustees, and Management Committee
- The Management Committee – to the Trustees, the Rules and Compliance Committee, the Finance Committee, Area Representatives and Branch Operations Directors
- The Safety and Welfare Advisory Committee – to the Trustees, Area Representatives and Branch Operations Directors
- The committees established under these Rules – to the Management Committee, the Rules and Compliance Committee, Area Representatives and Branch Operations Directors

6.2 Where a matter which is confidential (by reason of data protection legislation or otherwise) or the disclosure of which could prejudice the financial interests of The Pony Club is included in the minutes of any meeting, a summarised version of the minute omitting such details as will remove that prejudice, may be distributed to the relevant persons provided that the minute includes an indication of the general nature of the matter discussed.

7. MEMBERSHIP

Eligibility

7.1 Membership is available to anyone until the end of the Membership Subscription year in which he becomes 25 years old. Membership may be as a Branch Member or as a Centre Member. Membership as a Branch Member may be as a Riding Member or Non-Riding Member.

7.2 Where membership is of a Branch, a Member cannot join more than one Branch at one time. Usually, Branches accept any application for membership from people resident within their Branch District.

7.3 Centre Membership is intended for anyone who does not have their own pony, (either owned, hired or on loan), who rides at a Pony Club Linked Riding Centre.

7.4 Centre Plus Membership is for anyone who rides at a Pony Club Linked Riding Centre and also has regular access to a horse/pony (whether owned by them, leased to them or loaned to them) to ride outside of Centre organised activities.

Termination of Membership

7.5 If the Renewal Subscription of any Branch Member has not been paid by the end of his Membership Subscription Year, membership is terminated from that date. As insurance cover will also cease at the same time, it is essential that a person whose membership has terminated must not be permitted to take part in any Branch or Centre activities, except those that are open to non-Members, until such time as he renews his membership of The Pony Club.

7.6 A District Commissioner may at any time recommend to their Branch Committee that they end the membership of any Branch

Member who, in the opinion of the District Commissioner, shows insufficient interest in their Branch.

7.7 A Branch Committee may make a Branch rule that Members, to participate in Branch activities, be selected to represent the Branch in any competition or be nominated to represent The Pony Club, should demonstrate an interest in and a commitment to the Branch unless prevented from doing so by illness, absence from home or any other reason which in the opinion of the District Commissioner justifies absence. In addition to demonstrating loyalty to the Branch, the combination of horse and rider may also be required to prove their competence and safety to compete at a certain level. The Rules and Compliance Committee may issue guidance to Branch Committees to the extent and type of rule that may be made under this provision.

7.8 An Area may make a rule that to be eligible to compete at Area Competitions, Members and/or their horse/pony must have actively taken part in a specified minimum number of Rallies/Qualifying Coaching/Training Sessions over a given period unless prevented from doing so by illness, absence from home or any other reason which in the opinion of the District Commissioner justifies absence. For the purposes of this rule a Rally/Qualifying Coaching/Training Session is one which is organised by a Branch Committee, the Area Representative or by the Training Committee and must be a minimum of one hour in length. Each day of a camp shall be counted as a separate Rally/Qualifying Coaching/Training Session.

7.9 Such a rule as is referred to in Rule 7.8 may only be made if a majority of the branches in the Area vote in favour of it at a meeting held under rule 9.16 below.

7.10 If it is proposed to end the membership of any Member, notice will be given to the Member after consultation with their Area Representative who then may make appropriate representations. The Chairman of The Pony Club or the Chief Executive may suspend any Member whose conduct is under investigation.

7.11 The Rules and Compliance Committee may expel or temporarily exclude from the benefits of membership, any Member whose conduct is such, in its opinion, as to be injurious or detrimental to the character or reputation of The Pony Club or of any of its Branches or Centres or to the interests of The Pony Club or its Members or whose conduct shall in the opinion of the Committee, make a Member unfit or unsuitable to continue as a Member. In the case of a Branch Member, the request for such an expulsion will be initiated by the decision of a Branch Committee to recommend to their Area Representative the expulsion of the Member. The Area Representative will then present the case to the Rules and Compliance Committee. In the case of a Centre Member, or Centre Plus Member an Area Centre Coordinator will recommend the expulsion to the Chairman of the Centre Membership Committee, who will present the case to the Rules and Compliance Committee.

7.12 Before the Rules and Compliance Committee expels or temporarily excludes a Member, he will be given reasonable notice of relevant meetings, and the full opportunity to defend himself, and to justify or explain his conduct. This will include making representations by way of defence, justification and explanation on behalf of the Member by his parents. If the Rules and Compliance Committee is of the opinion that the Member has been guilty of the alleged conduct and that the Member or parents of such Member has or have failed to justify or explain it satisfactorily, the Rules and

Compliance Committee shall decide either to expel or temporarily exclude the Member from The Pony Club.

7.13 The Rules and Compliance Committee may also terminate the membership of a Member on medical grounds, if it considers that the continuation of membership would be dangerous or detrimental to either the Member himself or to others. In reaching its decision, the Rules and Compliance Committee shall take into account such medical reports that may be available to it, but the absence of any medical reports shall not preclude the Rules and Compliance Committee from terminating the Member's membership.

7.14 Before the Rules and Compliance Committee terminates membership on medical grounds, the Member will be given reasonable notice of relevant meetings, and full opportunity to justify his continued membership. This will include making representations by way of justification and explanation on behalf of the Member by his parents and/or by appropriate medical professionals.

7.15 If a majority of the Rules and Compliance Committee present at the inquiry is of the opinion that the Member's medical condition satisfies the criteria specified above, then his membership will be terminated.

7.16 The Area Representative or the Chairman of the Centre Membership Committee (as appropriate) has the authority to suspend the Member from membership pending the Rules and Compliance Committee inquiry.

7.17 On the termination of membership for medical reasons, the Member will be entitled to a pro-rata refund of the subscription and/or fees paid for the current year.

7.18 A District Commissioner may refuse to accept an application for membership, or a request to transfer to his Branch. With the approval of the Area Representative, he may also refuse to renew the membership of a Member. Reasons for such action would normally be given.

7.19 If a District Commissioner refuses to renew a Member's membership, that person may apply to join another Branch. In such a case Rule 8 will apply,

7.20 On the ending of membership, whether because of age, non-payment of subscription, resignation, expulsion or any other reason whatever, the Member will forfeit all the privileges of membership and all rights against The Pony Club. Subscriptions will not, except as provided above, be returnable and the Member will still be liable for all annual subscriptions that had become due and remained unpaid at the date of ending of his membership.

Parents and Supporters

7.21 The Pony Club publishes on its website information on the role of parents and expects parents and those with parental responsibility to comply with the guidance set out.

7.22 Where the behaviour of a parent or supporter is considered to be detrimental to the conduct of Branch activities it may be necessary first to give a warning and ultimately (although The Pony Club may dispense with a warning in exceptional cases) to ban them from attending Pony Club activities. The parent or supporter should be informed of any such decision by means of a letter from the District Commissioner which should indicate the reasons for the decision and indicate that the parent or supporter can appeal against the warning to the Rules and Compliance Committee. Such appeal must be made within three weeks of receipt of the letter. They should also be informed that the Member with whom they are associated is still welcome at Pony Club activities and that the District Commissioner will indicate on entry forms to competitions run by other Branches that the parent has been banned from attending Pony Club activities.

8. BRANCH MEMBERSHIP AND TRANSFERS

Subscription

8.1 The Trustees will set the rate for the Annual Subscription and will publish this in the Handbook or on the website. They will also determine the capitation fee, which is that part of the Annual Subscription retained by the Pony Club Office or (as the case may be) paid by Branches to The Pony Club Office. A new Branch is exempted from paying the capitation fee in The Pony Club Year in which it is formed.

8.2 The first annual subscription is due when first applying for membership. Membership runs for twelve months from the date the subscription is received. A renewal reminder will be sent to the Member one month before the end of his Membership Subscription Year. Email Renewal reminders will be sent to the Member in the month leading up to the end of the Membership Subscription Year.

8.3 Applications for membership or to renew membership may be made online through the approved Pony Club portal or on the official Branch Membership Application Form. If Branches require additional information that is not included on the portal and form, this may be collected by means of a locally produced supplementary form, but this must be in addition to the official forms, not replacing them.

8.4 For the purposes of this Rule, a renewing Member is one who renews his membership and who has at any time in the past been a Member of any Branch of the Pony Club. His previous branch may not necessarily be the Branch that he is now applying to join.

8.5 A new Member is somebody who joins a Branch for the first time and has never previously been a Branch Member (although he could have been a Centre Member).

8.6 Family Membership is available up to a maximum of 5 children of the family (as defined in rule 2). Children to be covered by Family Membership must all live at the same permanent address and must be Members of the same Branch.

8.7 Where there is/are already one or two child/children in a family who are Members, and additional Children of the Family join or renew their membership, thereby meaning they would qualify for Family Membership, a new Family Membership for all the Children of the Family will be deemed to have commenced on the date of joining of the additional child(ren) which will terminate on the day before the anniversary of this date. The parent will then be liable to pay the then current Family Membership Fee less an amount equal to the proportion of the membership fees paid in respect of those children who were already members that is equivalent to the unexpired portion of each such member's Membership Subscription Year.

Visiting Members

8.8 All Members will be welcomed as occasional visitors at working rallies or other activities of a Branch/Centre other than their own Branch/Centre, provided that the agreement of both District Commissioners/ Centre Proprietors is obtained. A Visiting Member cannot represent the Branch/

Centre that he is visiting in any Pony Club competitions. He may not take tests (other than Achievement Badges) at that other Branch/Centre without the permission of his own District Commissioner/Centre Proprietor.

Transfers

Branch to Branch

8.9 Transfers between Branches are not encouraged, as The Pony Club believes they are not in the best interests of The Pony Club as a whole but any member wishing to transfer must submit a Transfer Request via the Pony Club Website. Before submitting a Transfer Request, the Member (if over 18) or the Member's parent in other cases must notify the District Commissioner of their current Branch of their wish to transfer.

8.10 Notice of all Transfer Requests between branches will be given to the Area Representative(s) and District Commissioner of both the current and proposed Branches. If the transfer is approved by the District Commissioner of the receiving Branch concerned it can go ahead. Otherwise the following shall apply.

8.11 a) If within 21 days of receiving notice of the proposed transfer, the receiving District Commissioner has not notified the Membership Team that he disagrees with the transfer, it shall be deemed to have been approved.

(b) If the proposed transfer is declined by the receiving District Commissioner, the matter will be referred to the relevant Area Representative who will seek to resolve the matter or identify another Branch willing to accept the Member. If the Area Representative is unable to do either of these things, the matter will be referred to the Rules and Compliance Committee.

(c) Unless otherwise agreed by the Rules and Compliance Committee, no member may transfer more than once in any period of three years. This rule shall not apply where the transfer results directly from a permanent change of residence into the district of the Branch to which the member wishes to transfer.

8.12 For the avoidance of doubt, Rules 8.9 to 8.11 do not apply to a Renewing Member if that Renewing Member has not been a member of The Pony Club at any time within the 24 months prior to the date of their application to re-join The Pony Club. The member should contact the office in the first instance so that the change of Branch can be made in Pelham as they cannot change it on the portal.

8.13 Individual Sports Committees shall have the power to establish rules in relation to the eligibility of members who have transferred to compete in that sport.

8.14 In the year of transfer no part of the Annual Subscription of a Member will be payable to the "receiving" Branch unless the Annual Subscription is paid to the "receiving" Branch after the transfer.

Other Transfers (Membership Changes)

8.15 All Membership Changes between Branches/Centres will be managed directly by the Membership Team in the Pony Club Office. Notice of any such change to or from a Branch will be given to the Area Representative and District Commissioner via the New Member Application process.

Branches outside the UK

8.16 The Rules of The Pony Club apply only to Great Britain and Northern Ireland.

8.17 Any Club situated outside Great Britain and Northern Ireland and having objects similar to those of The Pony Club may, with its approval, be affiliated to The Pony Club and when and so long as it is affiliated it must be known by a name indicating that it is a Branch of The Pony Club.

8.18 Any affiliated Club, Advisory Board or Committee will make any rules for its constitution and organisation as it shall think fit, but these rules must first be sent to and approved by The Pony Club who may require any amendments and additions and deletions as it thinks proper.

8.19 In any event approval will be withheld unless the rules incorporate the objects and spirit of the Rules of The Pony Club.

8.20 A Member of an affiliated Overseas Branch can transfer to a UK Branch and become a full Member. The same conditions will apply as for UK Members (see Transfer rule).

8.21 Affiliated Clubs will contribute an affiliation fee to The Pony Club, which will be set by the Trustees.

8.22 Any approval by The Pony Club given to Affiliated Clubs may at any time be withdrawn when all privileges will be terminated. Adequate notice will be given, along with reasons for withdrawal, in reasonable time. The Pony Club from time to time may also vary the conditions of membership and the Rules of Affiliated Clubs, upon reasonable notice.

9. AREA AND BRANCH ORGANISATION

Areas and Branches

9.1 The Pony Club's administration in the UK is divided into Areas, which are defined by the Area Representatives' Committee. Each Area will be headed by an Area Representative. Areas consist of a number of Branches and the Area Representative will agree the geographical boundary of each Branch. The creation of a new Branch, or the amalgamation of existing Branches, must have the prior agreement of the Area Representative. If a Branch cannot agree its boundaries with the Area Representative, it will have the right of appeal to the Management Committee. It is permissible for Branches to have overlapping boundaries.

9.2 Branches must follow the purposes of The Pony Club, as stated in Rule 1.1 and are governed by the Rules of The Pony Club.

9.3 The Rules and Compliance Committee shall have the power to suspend or expel a Branch or an officer or committee member of that Branch, if it believes there to be a breach of this requirement. Similar action may be taken if it believes that The Pony Club is being brought into disrepute.

9.4 Before the Rules and Compliance Committee suspends or expels a Branch, the District Commissioner and Branch Secretary will be given reasonable notice of relevant meetings, and full opportunity to defend the Branch and to justify or explain its conduct.

9.5 This will include making representations by way of defence, justification and explanation on its behalf. If the majority of the Rules and Compliance Committee present is of the opinion that the Branch is in breach of its obligations and that its representatives have failed to justify or explain it satisfactorily, the Rules and Compliance Committee shall decide either to suspend or to expel the Branch.

9.6 In the case of the proposed suspension or expulsion of an officer or committee member, they shall be entitled to similar notice periods and entitlement to defence.

Area Representatives

9.7 The District Commissioners in each Area will elect, from amongst themselves or from outside, an Area Representative. On a vacancy, or in June of the third year of an Area Representative's term, the Pony Club Office will ask the District Commissioners in that Area to nominate their choice, having confirmed that the person concerned is willing to stand. The Pony Club Office will then organise a vote. District Commissioners can nominate themselves.

9.8 The appointment of a person as Area Representative will be subject to confirmation by the Management Committee. They will hold office for three years from 1st January after the date of their election and will be eligible for re-election. They will represent their Area on the Area Representatives' Committee and will offer help and advice to District Commissioners and/ or their committees on the organisation and administration of the individual Branches in their Area.

9.9 The responsibilities of Area Representatives include:

- To ensure that their Branches are aware of and adhere to the Health and Safety and Safeguarding Policies, and other statutory obligations.
- To hold at least two Area Meetings per year.
- To co-ordinate with Branches and Centres in the Area the dates of competitions, coaching courses and training days and to arrange organisers, dates and venues for Area competitions.
- To find out the views and wishes of their Branches and represent those views when required to the Office.
- To liaise with appropriate committees and or members of staff.
- To pass to the Pony Club Office anything in the Area that requires its attention.
- To advise the Volunteers and Officials Committee of the suitability of new District Commissioners elected by Branches in their Area and of new Branches proposed in their Area.
- To handle complaints.
- To give, when appropriate, general advice, help and support to District Commissioners and Centre Proprietors and if necessary, to exercise supervision on;
    - The appointment of new District Commissioners
    - Branch problems
    - Branch programmes
    - Health and Safety and Safeguarding
- To advise on the accreditation of Coaches and Nominees for the Visiting Coaches Panel and National Assessors' Panel.
- To organise or delegate the responsibility of organising Area Training courses for Coaches, Assessors for 'AH' and 'B' Test levels, and candidates for the higher Tests as required by their Branches/Centres.
- To approve 'A' Test nominations.
- To have an up-to-date panel of Assessors for 'B' Tests and send it to The Pony Club Office each year.
- To organise, or delegate the responsibility for appointing, suitable 'B' Test Assessors to attend a study day to make sure there is a level standard of examining for the Test in the Area. Assessors should attend at least one study day every two years to remain on the Area Panel.
- To keep a record of passes at AH, B+ and all levels of 'B' Tests.
- To advise the Pony Club Office of any views from their Area on new riding establishments applying to become a Pony Club Linked Riding Centre.
- To assist Centre Proprietors to find Assessors for Pony Club Tests up to and including 'C+' Standard.
- To let the Pony Club Office know of any

suitable Members from their Area for overseas visits and other events.

- To inform the Pony Club Office of any suitable students for any nationally organised course, such as the 'A' Test Coaching Camp
- To ensure financial records are kept for any accounts held by the Area such that, Annual Accounts for Areas (including those for Area Sports) are sent to The Pony Club Office on the form provided. A completed Area Annual Financial Return submission will encompass:
    - Fully completed, balanced return signed by the AR or the delegated officer: and
    - Bank statements and building society pass books showing the balance as at 31st December.

Assistant to an Area Representative

9.10 An Area Representative may (after consulting with the District Commissioners in his area,) appoint a person as Assistant to the Area Representative to assist and support the Area Representative in carrying out his/her responsibilities. This may include:

- at the request of the Area Representative to attend various meetings and events within the Area on behalf of the Area Representative.
- to assist the Area Representative in organising Area meetings
- to maintain an up-to-date panel of Assessors for C+, B, B+ and AH Tests within the Area
- to organise the appointment of suitable Assessors to officiate at B, Lunge, B+ and / or AH Tests within the area.

to maintain financial records for the Area to enable the Area Representative to submit Annual Accounts to The Pony Club Office.

9.11 The appointment of a person as Assistant to the Area Representative shall be a personal one and the appointment shall terminate if for any reason the Area Representative who appointed him/her to the post ceases to be the Area Representative. In exceptional circumstances the Management Committee shall have the power to terminate the appointment of a person as Assistant to the Area Representative.

9.12 If an Area Representative loses the confidence of his District Commissioners, and he is unwilling to resign, then this should be reported to the Rules and Compliance Committee in writing and signed by a majority of the District Commissioners in the Area.

9.13 The Rules and Compliance Committee will appoint a person to investigate fully and, if necessary, to report. The Rules and Compliance Committee in its absolute discretion may end the appointment of an Area Representative at any time upon giving written notice to the individual.

9.14 The Rules and Compliance Committee will normally seek representations from the individual concerned and will give reasons for its decision. However, in certain circumstances (which it may in its absolute discretion determine) it may decide not to give reasons.

9.15 Area Representatives will be reimbursed expenses incurred by them in accordance with the Pony Club Expenses Policy.

Area Meetings

9.16 At least twice per year, Area Representatives will hold meetings with the District Commissioners (or their representatives) in their Area. If so wished, these may be open meetings. The purpose of these meetings shall be to provide a forum for debating areas of concern. Area

Representatives should obtain the views of their District Commissioners on these matters, whilst recognising the independence of individual Branches to conduct their own activities, subject to the ultimate authority of the Management Committee. One of the meetings shall be held in the autumn, prior to the Annual General Meeting.

District Commissioners

9.17 Each Branch will be managed by a Branch Committee chaired by its District Commissioner. The first District Commissioner of a new Branch will be appointed for three years by the Volunteers and Officials Committee on the recommendation of the Area Representative. Thereafter the District Commissioner will be appointed by the Branch Committee.

9.18 If a District Commissioner **takes office** before 1st July in the calendar year, his term will end at the third 31st December after the date of his appointment. If he is appointed after 30th June, his term will end at the fourth 31st December after the date of his appointment. A District Commissioner does not need to be a member of the Branch Committee before election.

9.19 When the term of office of a District Commissioner is due to expire, the Branch Committee will meet to arrange to elect his successor, although the retiring District Commissioner may offer himself for re-election. If he is offering himself for re-election, the retiring District Commissioner cannot vote in this election, and must retire from the meeting whilst the election and votes take place.

9.20 If the retiring District Commissioner is not standing for re-election then he does not have to retire from the meeting and will continue to act as Chairman of the Branch Committee until the end of his period of office. If the District Commissioner is not present and the Branch has appointed an Assistant District Commissioner who is present, he will chair the meeting, otherwise the members of the Branch Committee present at that meeting will appoint a person present to act as Chairman for the election. In the event of an equality of votes, the person chairing the meeting will have a casting vote.

9.21 In the event of there being more than one candidate for District Commissioner, the election will be by secret ballot and it will be the responsibility of the Branch Secretary to provide a sufficient number of ballot papers for each Committee member present to vote. All candidates nominated for District Commissioner will retire from the meeting when the ballot is taking place and will not return until all the votes have been counted and the result given to the person chairing the meeting. Candidates will not have a vote.

9.22 A newly elected District Commissioner will take office on the next 1st January, unless the position of District Commissioner is vacant, in which case he will take office immediately.

9.23 A retiring District Commissioner may not serve as a Committee member of the same Branch for a period of one year from the date of his retirement except in exceptional circumstances and with the approval of the Rules and Compliance Committee.

9.24 The appointment of the District Commissioner elected will be subject to the approval of the Volunteers and Officials Committee which will take the opinion of the Area Representative into account. If the new District Commissioner has not yet attended a **'Branch Officials'** Training Day, his appointment will be conditional, and will not be confirmed until he has attended such a day. If the new District Commissioner has not attended a 'Branch Officials' Training Day within 12 months of receiving conditional approval, his Area Representative must either revoke his appointment or grant him an extension of time. The maximum extension allowed is one further period of 12 months. Until the approval and training process is completed, a new District Commissioner will function in an acting capacity.

9.25 In exceptional circumstances, and at the discretion of the Volunteers and Officials Committee, Joint District Commissioners of a Branch may be appointed. However, in this event, one of the District Commissioners must agree to accept the ultimate responsibility for carrying out the duties and responsibilities of a District Commissioner, as detailed in Rule 9.30 below.

9.26 Normally a person who is an Equestrian Professional will not be eligible for appointment as a District Commissioner. The Volunteers and Officials Committee however, at its absolute discretion, may decide to approve the appointment of an Equestrian Professional as a District Commissioner and may attach to the approval such conditions as the Volunteers and Officials Committee in its absolute discretion considers appropriate. In such a case, the person must submit a written declaration that he has read and understood the Conflict of Interest Policy of The Pony Club, as defined in Rule 5 and that he will adhere to it.

9.27 If any person ceases to be a District Commissioner for any reason, or if a District Commissioner elected by a Branch Committee is not approved by the Volunteers and Officials Committee, the Branch Committee will as soon as practical **(and in any event no later than 6 months after the position becomes vacant)** hold a committee meeting and will elect a District Commissioner to take the place of the existing one. The District Commissioner thus elected will hold office for three years. Such an election will be subject to the approval of the Volunteers and Officials Committee and the training process as detailed above.

9.28 The Volunteers and Officials Committee generally will, but is not required to, give reasons for not giving its approval of the appointment of a District Commissioner elected by a Branch Committee. It may allow representations from the candidate.

9.29 A District Commissioner is not allowed to make cash or other financial contribution towards the expenses of his Branch. This does not preclude a District Commissioner from waiving repayment of his travelling or out of pocket expenses, if he so wishes.

9.30 The responsibilities of District Commissioners are to ensure that:

- The Branch complies fully with the Health and Safety and Safeguarding Policies, and other statutory obligations.
- They are familiar with The Pony Club's Health and Safety Rule Book and Safeguarding Policy and that a copy is given to every Camp Organiser
- **Training, rallies and camp are provided for all Members in all aspects of horsemanship and riding skills, providing an opportunity for the Members to progress through use of the Pony Club Badges and Tests. This may be delegated to a Senior Coach, or Rally Organiser (Committee Member)**
- The membership database for the Branch reflects the Members of the branch and any anomalies are reported to The Pony Club Office as soon as noted.

- Joining fees and Annual Subscriptions are collected.
- All returns and money required by the Rules are sent to the Pony Club Office according to the established timetable
- The names of Coaches used by the Branch, and their qualifications, are entered on the Coach Directory section of the Pony Club database.
- Minutes are taken of all Branch Committee Meetings and Annual Meetings and are kept.
- Simple financial accounts for the Branch are kept and arrangements made for the inspection of them if required by the Trustees or the Rules and Compliance Committee. A financial statement should be produced at each meeting of the Branch Committee.
- Accounts are audited yearly by an appropriate person or reviewed by a member of the Branch Committee who in either case is not related in any way to the Treasurer and does not live at the same address as the Treasurer.
- Annual accounts are sent to The Pony Club Office on the form provided. The accounts of all Sub- Committees, Parents' Associations or Support Groups must be included in the Branch Return.
- A register is kept of all the fixed assets (land, buildings, vehicles, caravans, trailers, jumps, trophies and other equipment belonging to the Branch, whether or not the Branch capitalises fixed assets in its accounts. Items costing or valued (whichever is the greater) less than £100 need not be entered on the register Property comprising a set should be priced as a set, not as individual items. This register must be physically checked at least once every year.
- The Branch Committee is made aware of all, important information from the Pony Club Office.
- Any other tasks and responsibilities that are given by the Management Committee are carried out.

The District Commissioner will usually delegate the following duties and responsibilities to the Branch Treasurer, but the District Commissioner is ultimately responsible to ensure :

- Appropriate financial records are kept as detailed in Rule 21.18.
- The Branch holds a bank account with at least 2 signatories
- Simple financial accounts for the Branch are kept and arrangements made for the inspection of them if required by the Trustees.
- A financial statement is produced at each meeting of the Branch Committee.
- Accounts are audited yearly by an appropriate person or reviewed by a member of the Branch Committee who in either case is not related in any way to the Treasurer and does not live at the same address as the Treasurer.
- Branch Financial Returns which include annual accounts are sent to The Pony Club Office on the form provided. The accounts of all Sub-Committees, Parents' Associations or Support Groups must be included in the Branch Return.
- A register is kept of all the fixed assets (land, buildings, vehicles, caravans, trailers, jumps, trophies and other equipment belonging to the Branch, whether or not the Branch capitalises fixed assets in its accounts. Items costing

or valued (whichever is the greater) less than £250 need not be entered on the register.

Property comprising a set should be priced as a set, not as individual items. This register must be physically checked at least once every year.

- Cash transactions are kept to a minimum as per Rule 21.25.
- Payments made to coaches and other camp helpers are done in line with rule 12.3.
- Expense payments made are in accordance with rules 12.4 and 12.5.

Branch Committee and Committee Members

9.31 The Branch Committee will consist of no fewer than five people including the District Commissioner and will be responsible for appointing the following Officers of the Branch: Branch Secretary, Branch Treasurer, Health and Safety Officer, and Branch Safeguarding Officer who will be members of the Branch Committee. **A person, including the District Commissioner, may hold more than one appointment, except no person may be appointed or reappointed as the Branch Secretary or the Branch Treasurer if that person resides at the same address as the District Commissioner or is a close family member of the District Commissioner.**

Additionally, the Committee may appoint an Assistant District Commissioner. A Branch Committee can at any time increase or reduce its number provided that it shall not be fewer than five. To do this or to fill vacancies, the Committee can at any time elect new members to join the Committee.

9.32 Persons appointed to Branch committees are expected to contribute fully to the working of that committee and therefore any persons who, without reasonable excuse, fails to attend (either in person or by conference call) three consecutive meetings of the committee shall cease to be a member of that committee.

9.33 No person may be appointed or re-appointed to the Committee of more than one Branch.

9.34 The appointment of all members of the Branch Committee will be for a fixed term and must be recorded in the minutes of the Committee. If appointed before 1st July in the calendar year, their term will end at the third 31st December after the date of their appointment. If appointed after 30th June, their term will end at the fourth 31st December after the date of their appointment. In either case a member of the Branch Committee may offer himself for re-appointment.

9.35 The Branch Committee will hold a meeting during the final three months of the year to elect persons to fill any vacancy arising at the end of that year by virtue of the expiry of the term of office of any member of the Branch Committee, although the retiring member may offer himself for re-election. If he is offering himself for re-election, the retiring member may not vote in this election, and must retire from the meeting whilst the election and votes take place.

9.36 If requested to do so by the Area Representative, a Branch shall supply to the Area Representative a list of all members of the Branch Committee and the date on which they were each appointed and if it appears to the Area Representative that a Branch has failed to hold elections in accordance with Rule 9.19 or 9.34, the Area Representative shall have power to suspend any member of the Branch Committee (including for the avoidance of doubt the

District Commissioner) until such time as the Area Representative is satisfied that an election to fill the post(s) has been conducted by the Branch in accordance with these rules.

9.37 In exceptional circumstances, after consultation with and with the approval of the Area Representative, a newly appointed District Commissioner who has attended a Branch Officials Training day, may require up to 50% of the Branch Committee to resign. **This power must be exercised within 6 months of the date on which the Volunteers and Officials Committee approves his appointment as District Commissioner.**

9.38 The District Commissioner will be the Chairman of the Branch Committee. However, if he is unable to be present at a Committee meeting, the Assistant District Commissioner (if appointed) will be the Chairman. Otherwise, the other members present shall choose one of their number to chair the meeting. The Branch Committee of each Branch will meet at least four times each year. A quorum will consist of not less than three members. Questions at any meeting will be decided by a majority vote. In the case of an equality of votes the Chairman will have a second or casting vote. If a member of the Branch Committee cannot attend a meeting, they cannot nominate an alternate person to attend on their behalf.

9.39 The Branch Treasurer must present an Income and Expenditure Account and a Balance Sheet for the previous Pony Club Year, for approval by the Branch Committee. This should be done no later than the first Branch Committee meeting after the end of the relevant Pony Club Year.

9.40 The accounting records of the Branch (including, but not limited to, ledgers, bank statements, invoices, cheque books and counterfoils, paying in books and counterfoils, pass books and computerised records) are the property of the Branch. Should the accounts be kept on a computer, then the rights to use any proprietary software (including serial numbers and activation codes) must be owned by the Branch. Accounting records kept in a computer must be securely backed up at regular intervals, at least monthly. If the computer system is password protected, the password must be known by another member of the Branch Committee as well as the Treasurer.

NB Regulation of charities has become increasingly strict, particularly in regard to the management of finances. A pamphlet "Guidelines for Branch Treasurers" is issued to all Branch Treasurers and District Commissioners and is also available on the website. This gives advice on the duties and responsibilities of Branch Treasurers

9.41 Should it appear that a Branch Treasurer or any other person carrying out the functions of a Branch Treasurer, or any other person performing financial functions for the Branch (such as cheque signing or handling cash), is not providing the required level of financial stewardship, the Rules and Compliance Committee may suspend them from office, and order that all of the Branch's financial records and documents should be surrendered to a named person. In the period between Rules and Compliance Committee meetings, the Treasurer of The Pony Club may initiate the suspension and if the official concerned is the Branch Treasurer he will, if required to do so by the Area Representative, surrender all of the Branch's financial records and documents to a named person pending the outcome of the matter.

9.42 The Rules and Compliance Committee shall order an investigation into the complaint against the suspended person. Depending on the outcome of this investigation, he may either be reinstated or removed from office. In the latter case, he shall have the right to appeal to the Appeal Committee, the decision of which shall be final.

9.43 If a Branch Committee passes a Vote of No Confidence in the District Commissioner or any other member of the Branch Committee, and he is unwilling to resign, then this will be reported to the Area Representative. The Area Representative will arrange for an investigation into the matter to be undertaken either personally or by some other person appointed by him and for the result of the investigation to be reported to the Rules and Compliance Committee for a decision as to whether to terminate the appointment of the individual concerned. Pending a decision by the Rules and Compliance Committee the District Commissioner or Branch Committee member concerned shall be suspended from acting in that capacity.

9.44 The Area Representative or the Rules and Compliance Committee may also initiate an investigation into the conduct of a District Commissioner or other Branch Committee member. The Committee may deem it appropriate that a person other than the Branch's Area Representative should carry out any investigation. The Rules and Compliance Committee, in its absolute discretion, may end the appointment of a District Commissioner or Branch Committee member at any time upon giving written notice, both to the individual and to the Branch Secretary. The Committee would normally seek representations from the individual concerned and would give reasons for its decision. However, in certain circumstances (which it may in its absolute discretion determine) it may decide not to give reasons.

9.45 A Branch Committee may create one or more sub-branches in outlying parts of the District covered by the Branch. These sub-branches will be managed by the Branch Committee who can appoint a sub-committee for that purpose. The District Commissioner and at least one other member of the Branch Committee will be members of any sub- committee or any Parents' Associations/ Support Groups, etc established.

9.46 The funds of any sub-branches, Parents' Associations, or any other Support Group and their use are under the control of the District Commissioner and the Branch Committee, and they may instruct that all or part of such funds shall be transferred to the Branch account.

Parents' Meeting

9.47 Each Branch must hold a Parents' Meeting annually, open to Parents and Members. As a minimum, the Parents' meeting must include a report from the District Commissioner on the activities of the past year, the presentation of a simple financial statement by the Treasurer, and questions and opinions from the floor. Other reports may be given as appropriate, and awards may be presented. The Parents' meeting has no authority to impose decisions on the Branch Committee but the Branch Committee shall in making any decision have due regard to any views expressed at a Parents' Meeting.

Branch Presidents

9.48 A Branch Committee may have a Branch President, but a person shall not by virtue only of being the President become a member of the Branch Committee. Branch Presidents shall serve for a three-year term, terminating at the third 31st December after the date of their appointment. They can be re- appointed by the invitation of the Branch Committee.

Amalgamation and closing of Branches

9.49 If the Management Committee, in its absolute discretion considers that a Branch has become so small as to be unable to provide an adequate quality or variety of activities to its Members or that the continued operation of the Branch will prejudice the effective, efficient and economic management of The Pony Club, the Management Committee may require the Branch to close or amalgamate with an adjoining Branch.

9.50 The Management Committee shall not exercise its power in Rule 9.49 to require a Branch **to close or** amalgamate with an adjoining Branch unless it has first given to the District Commissioner and Branch Secretary of both Branches, notice of its intention to do so. The notice may include details of any improvement(s) the Management Committee would consider a Branch needs to make to avoid the Management Committee taking such action and of any reasonable period within which such improvement(s) must be made. The District Commissioner and Branch Secretary will be given reasonable notice of relevant meetings, and full opportunity to present reasons why the Branch should not be amalgamated with an adjoining Branch.

9.51 If a Branch, for whatever reason, ceases to exist it is the duty of the District Commissioner, or if there is not a District Commissioner then of the Secretary of the Branch Committee, to send the following to The Pony Club Office: -

- All the funds of the Branch and of any sub branch(es) under the management of the Branch Committee.
- All the Branch membership records, including those of any sub-branch(es).
- All financial books and statements of the Branch and any sub-branch(es)
- The Minute Books of the Branch and of any sub-branch(es).
- All other significant documents held by the Branch and any sub-branch(es).

An inventory of all equipment held and owned by the Branch and any sub-branch(es).

9.52 The Management Committee shall decide the disposition of Branch equipment and assets, although it may delegate this decision to the Area Representative.

9.53 The Branch Secretary must send a copy of the minutes of every meeting of the Branch Committee and any subcommittee thereof to the Area Representative.

Branch in Special Measures

9.54 If an Area Representative believes that a Branch Committee:

- **is failing to operate in accordance with the Rules of The Pony Club,**
- **is not acting cohesively for the benefit of the Membership;**
- **is acting in a manner such that The Pony Club is likely to be brought into disrepute by their conduct or is otherwise concerned about the conduct of a Branch Committee,**

they may request the Management Committee to place the Branch in Special Measures.

9.55 Before the Management Committee places a Branch into Special Measures, the District Commissioner and Branch Secretary will be given reasonable notice of any meeting at which the matter is to be discussed and an opportunity to explain why the Management Committee should not do so.

Special Measures means that

(a) the Area Representative and/or a Branch Operations Director will attend and chair meetings of the

Branch Committee.

(b) no new appointments to the Branch Committee may be made without the approval of the Area Representative

(c) no decision may be made by the Branch Committee to commit to expenditure which exceeds £1000 without the agreement of the Area Representative

9.56 A Branch Committee may ask the Management Committee to come out of Special Measures if it establishes that

(a) measures have been put in place to ensure that it can and will operate in accordance with the Rules of The Pony Club including (but without prejudice to the generality thereof) measures to ensure that all members of the Branch Committee have been appointed in accordance with these Rules;

(b) the Branch Committee is working cohesively for the benefit of the Membership;

(c) that The Pony Club will not be brought into disrepute by their conduct.

(d) all members of the Branch Committee have completed a Branch Officials' Training Course

(e) all members of the Branch Committee have completed a Pony Club approved Safeguarding Course and have a current DBC/PVS/ AccessNI check; and

(f) all members of the Branch Committee have signed and returned a copy of the Code of Conduct for Officials Volunteers and Staff.

10. BRANCH ACTIVITIES

Scope

10.1 Branches have the right to arrange their own programme of activities, subject only to compliance with these Rules and to any directions that may be given by the Area Representatives Committee or the Management Committee. A Branch Programme, listing forthcoming activities approved by the District Commissioner, should be given to all Members at regular intervals.

10.2 A Branch will not hold an activity in the District of any other Branch (unless it is in shared territory) except by invitation or permission of the other District Commissioner. This should not unreasonably be refused. This Rule shall not apply to commercial premises.

Welfare

10.3 At Pony Club activities, the following are unacceptable: -

- ponies that are aged under four years.
- ponies that are infirm through old age;
- ponies that are ill, thin or lame;
- ponies that are a danger to their riders or to other Members or their ponies;
- mares that are heavy in-foal, mares in milk and mares with foal at foot;

obese ponies.

10.4 Stallions can only be ridden at Pony Club events by Members if they obtain written permission from their District Commissioner and must wear identifying discs on their bridle in the interests of safety.

10.5 All ponies are expected to be properly groomed and well turned out, with correctly fitting tack.

10.6 If Branches incur expenses to pay for Coaches and/or facilities, it is permissible to charge Members a commensurate fee for attendance at an activity. Membership of The Pony Club does not confer any right to free rallies, although these may be given if funds permit.

Rallies / Coaching / Training Sessions

10.7 Nobody can organise a Branch Rally/ Coaching/Training Session or coach at a Branch Coaching/Training Session unless authorised by the District Commissioner.

Practices

10.8 Practices for the various sport competitions shall be announced in the Branch Programme, so that all eligible Members wishing to take part may do so. Any additional practices that are arranged within the period covered by the current Branch Programme, but after the Programme has been distributed, must have the approval of the District Commissioner.

Pony Club Camps

10.9 A Camp is an assembly of The Pony Club Members, together with ponies, held over a period of several days, usually during the summer holidays. It may be either residential or non-residential for both Members and ponies. The object of Camp is to provide an instructional holiday for Members and their ponies. Training should be given each day, but the holiday element must not be neglected and there should be a balanced mix of enjoyable activities and competitions. Not all of these activities and competitions need to be equestrian in nature. Camp is intended to be fun.

10.10 In view of the additional responsibilities for the Health, Safety and Safeguarding of the Members that arise from its very nature, Camp, and particularly residential Camp, must be very carefully organised. Rigorous Risk Assessments must be carried out at all venues to be used, and the person in charge of the Camp (the Camp Organiser) must be fully conversant with The Pony Club's Health and Safety Rule Book and Safeguarding Policy. Camp Organisers should be given guidance on supervision levels and safeguarding, particularly at night.

10.11 A responsible adult must be available to the Members at all times of the day and night. There must also be a trained First Aider equipped with a mobile telephone and an appropriately stocked First-Aid Kit. Arrangements for catering must ensure that all food hygiene regulations are fully met.

Competitions

10.12 A Branch may organise competitions in any of The Pony Club's sports. These competitions can either be restricted to the Branch's own Members, restricted to Pony Club Members or open to the general public. All competitions organised by Pony Club Branches shall be conducted under the Rules as printed in the applicable Sport Rule Book, unless otherwise stated in the schedule of classes and regulations published for the competition.

10.13 Cash or other valuable prizes must not be given at Pony Club competitions. Prizes should normally take the form of rosettes and/ or trophies.

Other Activities

10.14 A Branch can arrange other activities for its Members and their families such as a Quiz, outings, social events and fund-raising events. These other activities do not need to be equestrian in nature.

11. CENTRE AND CENTRE PLUS MEMBERSHIP

Purpose and Scope of Activities

11.1 Centre Membership is intended to enable someone who only rides a Centre owned horse/pony during a Centre organised activity to become a Member of The Pony

Club. Centre Members are able to take part in all Pony Club activities.

11.2 Centre Plus Membership is for Members who ride at a Centre and also have regular access to ride a horse/pony outside of Centre organised activities. The Centre Plus Membership fee will be equal to the Branch Membership fee. Transfers between Centres and Branches will be handled by the Membership team at The Pony Club office on completion of a CentrePlus transfer request.

11.3 Centre Members and Centre Plus Members are eligible to participate in all sports and competitions open to Members, although the Centre Equitation competition is for Centre Members only.

11.4 Centre and Centre Plus Members have third party legal liability insurance cover.

Membership – Centre and Centre Plus

11.5 The Trustees will set the rate for the Annual Subscription and will publish this in the Handbook.

11.6 The first Annual Subscription is due when first applying for membership. The initial membership application must be endorsed by the Centre Proprietor.

11.7 Membership runs for twelve months from the date the subscription is received. A renewal reminder will be sent to the Member one month before the end of his Membership Subscription Year. Email Renewal reminders will be sent to the Member in the month leading up to the end of their Membership Subscription Year.

11.8 The Centre Membership Committee may expel any Member whose conduct is such, in their opinion, as to be injurious to the character or reputation of The Pony Club, to any of its Centres or to the interests of The Pony Club or Members or whose conduct shall in the opinion of the Centre Membership Committee, make a Member unfit or unsuitable to continue as a Member.

11.9 Before the Centre Membership Committee expels a Member, that will be given reasonable notice of relevant meetings, full opportunity to defend themselves and to justify or explain their conduct. This will include making representations by way of defence, justification and explanation on behalf of the Member by the parents. If the majority of the Centre Membership Committee present at the inquiry are of the opinion that the Member has been guilty of the alleged conduct and that the Member or parents of such Member has or have failed to justify or explain it satisfactorily, the Centre Membership Committee shall ask the Member to resign. If they do not resign the Centre Membership Committee will expel the Member from The Pony Club.

11.10 The Pony Club Office may refuse to renew the membership of a Centre Member or Centre Plus Member. Reasons for such action would normally be given.

11.11 On the ending of membership, either because of age, non-payment of subscription, resignation, expulsion or any other reason whatsoever, the Member will forfeit all the privileges of membership and all rights against The Pony Club.

11.12 Subscriptions and/or fees will not in such circumstances be returnable and the Member will still be liable for all annual subscriptions and/or fees that had become due and remained unpaid at the date of ending of the membership.

Area Centre Coordinators

11.13 The duties and responsibilities of an Area Centre Coordinator are:

- To assess all riding schools who apply to become a Pony Club Centre and report their findings to The Pony Club Office.

- To contact each of the existing Pony Club Centres in their Area annually and report their findings to The Pony Club Office.
- To be a point of contact for the Centres in their Area for advice and assistance with Pony Club Tests and other aspects of Pony Club within the Centre.
- To liaise with the Area Representative
- To assist The Pony Club Office and Area Representative in communicating national or regional events, qualifying competitions and training opportunities to the Pony Club Centres.

Pony Club Centres

11.14 When a Riding Centre Proprietor applies to join the scheme, the Area Representative will be informed and the Riding Centre will be visited by an Area Centre Coordinator.

11.15 Provided that The Pony Club Office is satisfied that the Centre meets the required standards, the Centre Proprietor will be invited to enter into a legal agreement regulating the relationship between himself and The Pony Club. The Riding Centre will become known as The xxxxxx Pony Club Centre and its participation in the scheme will be renewable annually through an affiliation fee.

11.16 The Centre Membership Committee may recommend the withholding or termination of a Centre's participation in the Centre Membership Scheme at any time if the Centre is unable to provide, or ceases to provide, the benefits of Centre Membership as determined in Rules 11.1 and 11.2 above, or ceases to meet the standards required by The Pony Club. Adequate notice will be given, along with reasons for withdrawal, in reasonable time.

11.17 Pony Club Centres will display a Pony Club Centre plaque.

11.18 All Pony Club Centres must hold a current licence under the Riding Establishments Acts 1964 and 1970 or The Riding Establishments Regulations (Northern Ireland) 1980 or The Animal Welfare (Licensing of Activities Involving Animals) (England) Regulations 2018 (as appropriate).

11.19 All Pony Club Centres must have current Public Liability Insurance Cover, which must include cover for all their Pony Club activities. Members riding Centre owned ponies will be covered by The Pony Club Third Party Legal Liability Insurance Policy when taking part in any Pony Club activity. However, the pony itself will not be covered by this Insurance.

11.20 Pony Club Centres are required to provide the benefits of membership, including mounted and dismounted instruction to Members.

Pony Club Tests at Pony Club Centres

11.21 The Centre Proprietor must contact his Area Centre Coordinator, Area Representative and/ or the local District Commissioner if necessary, in order to find suitable Assessors for the Test to be taken at E, D, D+, C or C+ Standard. Thereafter, the Centre Proprietor must consult the Area Representative as to how and where further Tests are to be taken.

11.22 The riding component of the C Test must be taken outside and not in an indoor school.

11.23 It will be the responsibility of the Centre Proprietor to order any badges, felts, and certificates for presentation to successful candidates.

11.24 The Centre Proprietor or Test Organiser should update the Membership Database with badge and test results.

11.25 Candidates may be charged a fee by the Centre to cover the cost of Assessors' expenses, normal hire charges, and other costs.

12. REMUNERATION AND EXPENSES

Remuneration

12.1 No Trustee shall receive remuneration from The Pony Club in any circumstances. No Area Representative nor any District Commissioner shall receive any salary or emolument from The Pony Club or any of its Branches for performing his normal function within The Pony Club. However, the Management Committee shall have authority to waive this Rule for Area Representatives and District Commissioners in exceptional circumstances, in order to employ the particular skills of an individual for a specific purpose and provided that such payment is legally permissible.

12.2 Applications for such a waiver should be sent to the Chief Executive, in writing, giving precise details of the work to be done and the remuneration to be paid.

Payment of Coaches and others

12.3 Coaches and others such as Camp helpers may be paid a fee on production of an invoice. It is strongly recommended that fees should be negotiated in advance, and that they should not be paid in cash. Those paid fees may be members of Branch Committees but cannot be the District Commissioner unless he has received a dispensation from the Volunteers and Officials Committee under Rule 9.26.

Expenses

12.4 Travelling and out of pocket expenses of Trustees and, members of committees will be refunded by The Pony Club Office in accordance with the Pony Club Expenses Policy. Expense claims must be submitted to The Pony Club Office within 30 days from the end of the month of which the expense was incurred.

12.5 Branches may also reimburse such expenses incurred by District Commissioners, Branch Officers, Committee members and others acting on behalf of the Branch. Branches may, if they wish, pay a flat sum or a rate per capita to their District Commissioner, but they should be aware that the Inland Revenue may require the District Commissioner to justify the amount paid. Travelling expenses will be paid at either the Standard Class train fare or at the currently approved mileage rate if travelling by car. This rate should be used as the normal allowance for all Pony Club meetings and events. However, when using qualified officials (i.e. British Dressage judges or BS judges) their official rate should be paid.

13. THE PONY CLUB TESTS

13.1 Details regarding conditions of tests and badges can be found in the Administrative Notes section of the Handbook and online at pcuk.org.

13.2 Subject to rule 13.3, all mandatory tests must be taken in order.

13.3 In exceptional circumstances, an Area Representative, at the request of a District Commissioner or Centre Proprietor, may grant permission for a Member to omit taking a test before progressing to the next highest test.

14. COACH AND INSTRUCTOR ACCREDITATION

14.1 The Pony Club accredits its coaches and instructors in line with the detailed notes laid out in the "Coaches and Training" section of the Administrative Notes in the Handbook and on the website. The Pony Club grants this accreditation to coaches and instructors, and reserves the right to remove or suspend the accreditation of any coach or instructor if it considers it necessary. If a coach or instructor has their accreditation removed or suspended, they may not instruct for any Pony Club Branch or Centre until their accreditation is reinstated.

15. THE PONY CLUB CHAMPIONSHIPS

15.1 Each year, the Management Committee will appoint a Championships Committee to arrange a championship for each of the sports. Wherever possible, all of the sports will hold their championships at the same venue during August, but it is recognised that some sports may have to hold their own separate championships. Qualification for the championships will be through competitions held by each Area. In some sports, these Area competitions may be replaced or augmented by Zone competitions, in which two or more Areas combine.

15.2 The rules for each competition will be approved by the relevant committee for each sport.

16. DRESS AND SADDLERY FOR PONY CLUB MEMBERS

Hats and Hair

16.1 Hair must be tied back securely, in a safe manner to reduce the risk of hair being caught and to prevent scalp injuries. Individual Sports may have additional rules.

16.2 It is mandatory for all Members to wear a protective helmet at all times when mounted with the chinstrap fastened and adjusted so as to prevent movement of the hat in the event of a fall. This rule defines the quality of manufacture that is required. The individual sports **may** also have additional requirements with regard to colour and type. It is strongly recommended that second hand hats are not purchased.

16.3 The current hat standards accepted by the Pony Club are detailed in the table below:

Hat Standard	Safety Mark
Snell E2016 & 2021 with the official Snell label and number	
PAS 015: 2011 with BSI Kitemark or Inspec IC Mark	
(BS) EN 1384:2023 with BSI Kitemark or Inspec IC Mark	
VG1 with BSI Kitemark or Inspec IC Mark	
ASTM-F1163 2015 & 2023 with the SEI mark	
AS/NZS 3838, 2006 with SAI Global Mark	

- **Note: Some hats are dual-badged with different standards. If a hat contains at least one compliant hat standard it is deemed suitable for competition, even if it is additionally labelled with an older standard.**
- **For cross-country riding including Eventing, Tetrathlon and Hunter Trials, together with Pony Racing (whether it be tests, rallies, competition or training) and Mounted Games competitions, a jockey skull cap must be worn with no fixed peak, peak type extensions or noticeable protuberances above the eyes or to the front, and should have an even round or elliptical shape with a smooth or slightly abrasive surface, having no peak or peak type extensions.**

Noticeable protuberances above the eyes or to the front not greater than 5mm, smooth and rounded in nature are permitted. A removable hat cover with a light flexible peak may be used if required.

- **No recording device is permitted (e.g. hat cameras) as they may have a negative effect on the performance of the hat in the event of a fall.**
- **The fit of the hat and the adjustment of the harness are as crucial as the quality. Members are advised to try several makes to find the best fit. The hat should not move on the head when the head is tipped forward. The Pony Club recommends you visit a qualified BETA (British Equestrian Trade Association) fitter.**
- **Hats must be replaced after a severe impact as subsequent protection will be significantly reduced. Hats deteriorate with age and should be replaced after three to five years depending upon the amount of use.**
- **Hats must be worn at all times (including at prize-giving) when mounted with a chinstrap fastened and adjusted so as to prevent movement of the hat in the event of a fall.**
- **For Show Jumping: hat covers, if applicable, shall be dark blue, black or brown only. Branch/Centre team colours are permitted for team competitions.**
- **For Dressage: hats and hat covers must be predominately black, navy blue or a conservative dark colour that matches the rider's jacket for Area competitions or above. The Pony Club Hat silk is also acceptable.**
- **For Mounted Games: hat covers, if applicable, shall be dark blue, black or brown only.**
- **The Official Steward / Organiser may, at his discretion, eliminate a competitor riding in the area of the competition without a hat or with the chinstrap unfastened or with a hat that does not comply with these standards**

Hat Checks and Tagging

16.4 The Pony Club and its Branches and Linked Centres will appoint Officials, who are familiar with The Pony Club hat rule, to carry out hat checks and tag each hat that complies with the requirements set out in the hat rule with a pink Pony Club hat tag.

16.5 Hats fitted with a pink Pony Club, British Eventing (BE) or British Riding Club (BRC) hat tag will not need to be checked on subsequent occasions. However, the Pony Club reserves the right to randomly spot check any hat regardless of whether it is already tagged.

16.6 Pony Club hat tags (Pink) are only available to purchase from The Pony Club Shop.

16.7 Tagging is an external verification of the internal label and indicates that a hat meets the accepted standards. The tag does NOT imply any check of the fit and condition of the hat has been undertaken. It is considered to be the responsibility of the Member's parent(s) / guardian(s) to ensure that their hat complies with the required standards and is tagged before they go to any Pony Club event. Also, they are responsible for ensuring that the manufacturer's guidelines with regard to fit and replacement are followed.

For further information on hat standards, testing and fitting, please refer to the British Equestrian Trade Association (BETA) website: British Equestrian Trade Association - Safety and your head (beta-uk.org)

Ties and Stocks

16.8 The Pony Club's colours are pale blue, gold and purple, and Members should wear the approved tie in these colours whenever attending a Pony Club activity, unless the wearing of a tie is inappropriate to that activity.

16.9 Recognising the wide age range of Members, there is also a dark blue tie, which may be worn by Members who have attained their 18th birthday. Alternatively, a plain white or cream stock may be worn with a black or navy jacket, or a coloured stock may be worn with a tweed hacking jacket. It is permitted to wear a Pony Club stock with any coloured jacket.

Badges

16.10 The official membership badge should be worn at all Pony Club activities when a jacket is worn.

16.11 Branches and Centres give Members a coloured felt showing the highest Test standard achieved by the Member. It should be worn behind the membership badge.

16.12 Cloth Achievement Badges should be sown on to the Branch or Centre sweatshirt.

Body Protectors

16.13 The Pony Club does not make the use of body protectors compulsory, except for all Cross Country riding, Arena Eventing and Pony Racing whether it be training or competition. For these activities a Body Protector must meet BETA 2018 Level 3 standard (blue and black label).

16.14 For general use, the responsibility for choosing body protectors and the decision as to their use must rest with Members and their parents. It is recommended that a rider's body protector should not be more than 2% of their body weight. When worn, body protectors must fit correctly, be comfortable and must not restrict movement. BETA recommends body protectors are replaced at least every three to five years, after which the impact absorption properties of the foam may have started to decline.

Air Jackets

16.15 When an air jacket inflates the sudden noise can startle horses in the immediate vicinity thereby causing difficulties for the other Members of a ride if used in a group ride in a confined area, e.g. an indoor school or outdoor manège. Air jackets are therefore not encouraged for group rides.

Medical Armbands

16.16 Medical armbands are advised if Members are not accompanied by a responsible adult, including hacking on roads and are compulsory for Pony Racing and for Endurance rides.

Clothing, Footwear and Stirrups

16.17 When mounted at Pony Club activities, Members should wear a riding jacket or Branch/Centre sweatshirt, jodhpurs with leather shoes or jodhpur boots or breeches and either leather or rubber riding boots, a suitable plain-coloured shirt with a collar and The Pony Club tie or a stock.

16.18 Only standard riding or jodhpur boots with a well-defined square cut heel may be worn. No other footwear will be permitted including wellington boots, yard boots, country boots, "muckers" or trainers. Boots with interlocking treads are not permitted, nor are the boots or treads individually. Laces on boots must be taped for Mounted Games only.

16.19 Plain black or brown half chaps may be worn with jodhpur boots of the same colour. Tassels and fringes are not allowed.

16.20 Stirrups should be of the correct size to suit the rider's boots. They must have 7mm (¼") clearance on either side of the boot. To find this measurement, tack checkers should move the foot across to one side of the stirrup, with the widest part of the foot on the tread. From the side of the foot to the edge of the stirrup should be 14mm.

There are now many types of stirrups marketed as "safety stirrups". All riders must ensure that their stirrups are suitable for their type of footwear, the activities in which they take part and that the stirrup leathers are in good condition.

16.21 There are no prescribed weight limits on metal stirrups. However, with the advent of stirrups of other materials, weight limits are seen to be given by manufacturers. Anyone who buys these stirrups should take particular note if weight limits are on the box or on the attached information leaflets.

16.22 Neither the feet, nor the stirrup leathers nor irons, may be attached to the girth, nor may the feet be attached to the stirrup irons.

It is strongly recommended that the design of the stirrup chosen allows the foot to be released easily in the event of a rider fall. Specific rules for individual sports can be found in the respective sports rulebooks.

Particular focus should be on ensuring that the boot and stirrup are the correct size for the rider taking part and used in line with the manufacturer's guidance.

For the avoidance of doubt, at Pony Club events:

- stirrups which connect the boot and the stirrup magnetically are not allowed
- Interlocking boot soles and stirrup treads are not allowed.

16.23 New clothing is not expected, but what is worn must be clean, neat and tidy. Jeans should not be worn when mounted except when specifically allowed by certain sports. Polo shirts in Branch colours are allowed at rallies and at camp.

Spurs

16.24 Spurs may be worn at Rallies and other events. Any misuse of spurs will be reported to the District Commissioner/Centre Proprietor, Area Representative and Training Chairman and riders who are reported will be recorded and monitored. Sharp spurs are not permitted. Only blunt spurs, without rowels or sharp edges, and spurs that have a smooth rotating ball on the shank may be worn. If the spurs are curved, the curve must be downwards and the shank must point straight to the back and not exceed 4 cm in length. The measurement is taken from the heel of the boot to the end of the shank.

Jewellery

16.25 The wearing of any sort of jewellery when handling or riding horse/pony is not recommended and if done at any Pony Club activity, is done at the risk of the member/ their parent/guardian. However, to stop any risk of injury, necklaces and bracelets (other than medical bracelets) must be removed as must larger and more pendulous piercings which create a risk of injury to the body part through which they are secured. For the avoidance of doubt a wristwatch, wedding ring, stock pin worn horizontally and/or a tie clip are permitted to be worn . It is recommended that stock pins are removed for cross country.

Competitions

16.26 Additional or different dress requirements for competitions may be specified in the Sport Rule Books, but otherwise, these Rules shall apply.

Saddlery

16.27 Grass reins and balance support reins are permitted to be used in activities. They must be loosely fitted and not restrict the pony. The height limit for jumping is 50 cm. Other than this, only saddlery permitted in the Sports Rule Books may be used at Pony Club Activities relating to that sport. Side reins are not permitted.

16.28 Other than this only saddlery permitted in the Sport Rule Books may be used at Pony Club activities relating to that sport.

Unsafe Tack

16.29 All tack must be clean, in a good state of repair, properly fitted and suitable for purpose. Tack inspections are routinely carried out at events and the organisers may prohibit participation in the event if they consider the tack to be inadequate or unsuitable. Specific sport rules are detailed in respective rulebooks.

Electronic Devices

16.30 Electronic devices (i.e. headphones, mobile phones, etc. enabling another person to communicate with the rider) are not allowed whilst the rider is competing. No recording device is permitted (e.g. hat/bridle cameras, etc).

17. SAFEGUARDING

17.1 The Pony Club believes that it is essential that children and young people are encouraged to take part in outdoor activities and sports as part of their development to adulthood. Their participation in sport must be in a secure, safe and fun environment and be protected from harm. The positive effects of involvement with horses can help develop self-esteem, teamwork and leadership. This can only take place if equestrian sport is effectively regulated and managed by well trained staff and volunteers.

17.2 The full Safeguarding Policy contains the necessary policies and procedures which should be implemented and adhered to, including but not limited to:

- The appointment of a Branch/Centre Safeguarding Officer
- Dealing with safeguarding concerns and allegations
- Safer recruitment practices, including requirements for those carrying out regulated activity/work

17.3 As a member body of British Equestrian (BEF), in applying our Safeguarding Policy, we will follow the BEF Case Management Policy (with any necessary modifications). This Policy includes a provision allowing for the temporary suspension of an individual during an investigation.

18. DISPLAYS

18.1 Branches will not give displays, or stage competitions, at shows or other public gatherings without first obtaining the permission of their Area Representative.

19. PROHIBITED ACTIVITIES

19.1 Because of the risks involved, team-chasing events or practices must not be organised by The Pony Club, nor should Branch teams be entered in such events. The same restriction applies to Racing, other than racing sanctioned by The Pony Club Racing Committee. Team-chasing and other unauthorized racing is not covered by Pony Club insurance.

20. COMPLAINTS PROCEDURE

Competition Complaints and Objections

20.1 Complaints and objections arising from within competitions should be dealt with in accordance with the procedure detailed in the relevant sport rule book.

Decisions made in this way are final, and no appeal will be entertained. Should a breach of eligibility subsequently be discovered, then the Sport Committee may disqualify the offending team or individual. If the said individual was a member of a qualifying team, and their score contributes to the qualification, the team will be disqualified unless the qualification holds up using the discard score. In the event of disqualification, the next best placed team or individual will be promoted. Decisions made by the Sport Committee shall be final. No issue of eligibility can be considered after the Championship competition has been held.

Other Complaints and Problems

20.2 If a problem arises within a Branch or a Centre, it is for the District Commissioner or Area Centre Coordinator to try initially to resolve the problem. If they are unable to do so, then they should enlist the help of the Area Representative, who will consult with the relevant Committee Chairmen if necessary. If the problem still cannot be resolved, then the Area Representative (with the assistance of a Branch Operations Director if required) will refer the matter to the Rules and Compliance Committee, whose decision will, subject to Rule 20.3 be final. The decision will be advised to the complainant in writing.

20.3 The Rules and Compliance Committee may in exceptional circumstances and in cases where the Committee is unable to determine the matter properly due to a conflict of interest arising must, ask the Vice Chairman to establish an Appeals Committee under Rule 4.33 to review the matter and make a decision on it.

20.4 Any appeal to the Appeals Committee will be considered only after the above procedure has been carried out. If the complainant wishes to lodge an appeal, they must do so within **21** days of the date of the decision letter. They must also pay a deposit to The Pony Club Office. This deposit will be refunded if the appeal is upheld. The amount of the deposit will be shown in the Handbook.

21. FINANCE

21.1 Branches shall be largely autonomous in their control of Branch funds. However, it should be understood that, under charity law, the funds of The Pony Club, whether they are held by the Branches or by The Pony Club Office, are all part of The Charity. This means that, if any part of The Pony Club cannot pay its debts, payment must be made from elsewhere in The Pony Club. For this reason, a Branch may not, without the approval of the Finance Committee, enter into a financial commitment that risks a loss of a sum which is greater than £5,000 or the sum equal to 50% of its free reserves at the time of the commitment, whichever is the lesser amount.

21.2 A Branch that wishes to assign Designated Funds must obtain the consent of the Finance and Risk Committee.

21.3 Any purchase or rental of land (irrespective of value), and any capital expenditure in excess of £10,000, requires the prior approval of the Trustees. This requirement does not apply to casual hiring of facilities, provided that the hire period does not exceed one month. A Branch does not have the legal capacity to buy or rent land or buildings in its own name. All such transactions must be in the name of "The Pony Club", with the interest of the Branch being noted. All costs incurred, such as legal fees, are to be paid by the Branch.

21.4 Legally, The Pony Club is a charitable company, governed by its Memorandum and Articles of Association. In order to comply with the Memorandum and Articles, Pony Club funds may only be deposited with or lent to an institution, such as a bank or building society, which is regulated by the Financial Conduct Authority.

21.5 Bank Accounts

- Branches should use online banking provided that the Bank has a feature that requires two separate people to authorise transactions. For branches where this is not currently possible they should transition to a new account. In the interim paper statements should be obtained at least monthly and presented at every branch meeting.
- As a minimum, the Treasurer and District Commissioner should be signatories on the account. It is recommended that other officers are also made signatories in order that payments are not held up due to unavailability of the Treasurer or District Commissioner.
- The Treasurer and District Commissioner should review the account regularly and at least monthly
- All bank payments, both online and paper cheques require two signatories.
- Disbursements may not be made by telephone banking.
- Debit cards may be used but the Treasurer may not be the holder of a Debit Card. All holders must give the transaction dockets to the Treasurer at not greater than monthly intervals, together with an explanation of the reason for each purchase. The Treasurer will review these and report any anomalies to the District Commissioner or Area Representative.
- Credit cards are not allowed.

Building Society Account

If the Branch has a building society account, the Treasurer must bring the pass book to every committee meeting and make it available for inspection and must get the balance updated as at the year end.

21.6 These rules relate to all sub-groups, such as Parents' Associations and Sports Sub-committees that belong to the Branch.

Online Payment Systems

21.7 The use of online payment systems such as PayPal, Worldpay, Sagepay by Branches is permitted. However, it should be used in accordance with the relevant rules laid out in The Pony Club's Treasurer Guidelines, which are available on the Treasurers and Finance section of the website.

Returns to The Pony Club Office

21.8 To comply with charity law, all Branches are required to submit an Annual Financial Return to the Pony Club Office by **31st January** following the end of The Pony Club Year. Failure to do this will result in fines being imposed on The Pony Club, which will be recharged to the Branch(es) concerned. Invoices will be raised for any fines and sent to the branch pcuk.org email address.

21.9 The funds of all sub-branches, Parents' Associations and other sub-groups must be reported, either separately, or consolidated with the Branch. Funds held by Areas will also be reported.

21.10 Memberships are processed centrally at the Pony Club Office and via the Membership portal. Family Memberships have to be processed manually at The Pony Club Office. In case of an emergency and the Portal is unavailable, Branches can either use the "taster" rally option or a membership form should be emailed to Membership@pcuk.org before the event takes place and will be processed on the first following working day. Membership forms can now be completed electronically. At the end of each month a payment will be made to the Branch bank account by Direct Debit in respect of memberships taken during the month. Branches must ensure that a Direct Debit mandate is in place and kept up to date. Changes must be notified to the Pony Club Office.

21.11 For the purposes of the capitation

returns and the capitation fees, a Member who transfers from one Branch to another during The Pony Club Year shall be reported by the Branch to which he has paid his subscription. He should be excluded completely from the Return of the other Branch. Capitation is paid at the joining Branch and no subsequent adjustment can be made.

21.12 The annual financial return is due by the specified due date. Late submissions will incur a 'late submission fee'. If it is still outstanding one month after the specified due date, a further late submission fee will be incurred.

The fee(s) will be published in the Handbook or on the website. The invoice for the fee will be addressed to the District Commissioner of the Branch or for Area returns the relevant Area Representative and will be sent to their respective @pcuk.org email address.

A completed Branch Annual Financial Return submission will encompass:

- Fully completed, balanced return including a completed declaration signed by the Treasurer
- Bank statements and building society pass books showing the balance as at 31st December
- Fixed Asset Register

21.13 If the return is not received within 28 days from the date of the invoice for the fine, the Branch and/or one or more of its Officers or Committee members may be suspended from membership of The Pony Club until such time the Return is received. If a Return or Report has to be returned to a Branch because it contains errors, the Branch will remain in default until the satisfactorily corrected Return or Report (together with any payment that may be due) is received at The Pony Club Office. The Pony Club Office can also withhold future Direct Credits until payment is received.

The Chairman of The Pony Club has discretion to waive this Rule if he is satisfied that there are sufficient extenuating circumstances.

21.14 Following consultation with the Area Representative, the Management Committee may impose different reporting requirements upon Branches that are persistently late in filing their Returns.

21.15 It is a requirement of The Pony Club insurers that a list of the Members covered by public liability insurance can be made available to them if required. To satisfy this requirement, all Branches must submit details of their current membership by means of the online Database.

21.16 In the event that a Branch is unable to complete its Annual Financial return it may request the Pony Club Office to undertake the task for it. If a Branch makes such a request it must supply to the Pony Club Office: -

- A completed and balanced cashbook in either electronic or hard copy
- Copies of all bank statements for the year

If a branch does not have a cash book there will be an additional charge payable by the branch.

21.17 If a request is made to the Pony Club Office to complete an Annual Financial return the Branch will pay to the Pony Club Office a fee calculated in accordance with the following: -

- If the request is made prior to 9th January a fee of £5.00 per Member
- If the request is made on or after 9th January a fee of £7.50 per Member

An additional charge of £5.00 per member will be incurred to complete the cashbook.

Record Keeping

21.18 It is the responsibility of the Branch Treasurer to keep appropriate financial records. This must include:

- All financial transactions must be recorded in the cashbook (electronic / hardcopy), this includes recording the VAT that has been paid on each payment as per the receipt
- All payments made must have a receipt (can be scanned)
- Accounts packages such as Sage, Xero etc can be used
- All expenses claimed must have appropriate receipts attached

All records must be kept for a period of 6 years.

Branch Audits

21.19 The Pony Club Office may at any time request to audit the last two years of the Annual Financial Return of a Branch. Within 30 days of receiving an audit request the Branch Treasurer must send to the Pony Club Office the following documents: -

- Monthly Bank statements for all bank accounts held by the Branch for the period requested
- Download of all online payment platform transactions during the period requested
- A copy of the cashbook
- All receipts to evidence expenditure

21.20 Results of the audit will be communicated back to the Branch District Commissioner and Area Representative.

Branch Correspondence

21.21 All correspondence relating to Financial matters will be undertaken through the treasurer.branch@puck.org and copied to the dc.branch@pcuk.org email addresses.

Refunds

21.22 No refunds after close of entries.

21.23 Withdrawal before close of entries will get a full refund less a £10 admin fee (to be retained by The Organiser. This rule excludes Polo. See sport rule)

21.24 In the event of a competition being abandoned, for whatever reason, a refund of 50% of the entry fee will be given.

Cash

21.25

- In order to mitigate the risk associated with holding cash, cash transactions should be kept to a minimum.
- All cash handled by staff and volunteers, must be dealt with so as to ensure its safe custody and mitigate against loss whether through fraud, misappropriation or mistake. All payments made in cash must be supported by a receipt or other form of documentation to support the payment, must be recorded in a petty cash book and should be reviewed and authorised by someone other than the person who is maintaining the petty cash.
- A record of all cash received should be made in the petty cash book along with sufficient detail.
- Receipts should be issued for all cash received into petty cash. For fund raising activities such as raffles, one receipt for the total amount is sufficient but the receipt should detail the activity and individual giving the money.
- A regular and independent check of the petty cash float and records must be undertaken.

Direct Debits and Direct Credits

21.26

- Branches must maintain an up to date Direct Debit Mandate and must notify the Pony Club Office of any amendments
- Branches will be notified of payments

being made to the Branch or payments being made by the Branch relating to subscriptions and invoices raised by The Pony Club Office at least 10 days prior to the payment being made / taken.

- Any payments which are not regarding membership will have been invoiced in the month prior to the payment being taken and will have been sent to the branch pcuk.org email.

21.27 In order to safeguard individuals and to protect the funds of the Pony Club, the BranchCommittee/District Commissioner shall ensure that controls are in place to mitigate the risk of loss of the assets of the branch (whether through fraud, misappropriation or mistake).

21.28 The Pony Club Office may issue guidance to Branch Treasurers to assist them in performing their duties. This guidance must be followed and can be found on the website.

22. INSURANCE

22.1 The Pony Club has Insurance under a number of headings and policies, a summary of which is provided in the Handbook. In particular, all Branch and Centre Members are covered for their legal liability for accidental injury or damage to third parties or their property, arising out of the use or ownership of ponies at any time, not just on Pony Club activities. A full policy summary is shown on The Pony Club website.

22.2 Members and their parents must read the summary of cover carefully, to ensure that it satisfies their own requirements. It must be understood that this is liability Insurance and does not cover property belonging to, or in the care of, the Member or his family. Nor does it cover injury to the Member or his family. To comply with insurance requirements, all employees of The Pony Club (including contractors), paid and unpaid officials, instructors, volunteers, parents, Members of The Pony Club and visitors must: -

- Take all reasonable care for the Health and Safety and Welfare of themselves and others that may be affected by their actions or omissions.
- Co-operate fully with The Pony Club and its Officials on all Health and Safety and Safeguarding issues.
- Not intentionally or recklessly interfere with or misuse anything provided in the interests of Health and Safety.
- Use correctly and as intended all work items, procedures and personal protective equipment provided by The Pony Club (or other employers), in accordance with the training and instructions given and report any loss or defect immediately.
- Inform the District Commissioner or activity organiser of any situation they consider represents danger or could result in harm to themselves or others.
- Inform the District Commissioner or activity organiser of any failings or shortcomings as regards Health and Safety and Welfare.
- Report accidents either by making an entry in The Pony Club Accident Book or by informing the District Commissioner or activity organiser.

22.3 Insurance claims made by Branches are subject to an insurance excess, this excess may be recharged back to the Branch. This is £1,000.

23. LEGAL LIABILITY

23.1 Save for the death or personal injury caused by the negligence of the organisers, or anyone for whom they are in law responsible, neither the organisers of this event or The Pony Club nor any agent, employee or representative of these bodies, nor the landlord or his tenant, accepts any liability for any accident, loss, damage, injury or illness to horses, owners, riders, spectators, land, cars, their contents and accessories, or any other person or property whatsoever. Entries are only accepted on this basis.

24. GENERAL

24.1 Every eventuality cannot be provided for in these Rules. In any unforeseen or exceptional circumstances, it is the duty of the relevant officials to make a decision in the spirit and ethos of The Pony Club and to adhere as nearly as possible to the intention of these Rules.

Administrative Notes

PURPOSE

The Pony Club is a voluntary youth organisation for young people interested in ponies and riding. It has Branches and Centres worldwide but these notes apply only to the United Kingdom of Great Britain and Northern Ireland. Within the UK, it is a Registered Charity, and is subject to Charity legislation and to regulation by the Charity Commission.

The Pony Club's Charitable Purpose is:

- To promote and advance the education and understanding of the public and particularly children and young people, in all matters relating to horsemanship and the horse.
- To encourage the development of sportsmanship, unlocking potential by building resilience, confidence, teamwork and leadership skills.
- To support and develop the volunteering network to strengthen The Pony Club community and sustain life-long engagement with equestrianism.

The Pony Club has been granted constituent Membership of the National Council of Voluntary Organisations (NCVO). This means that The Pony Club is officially recognised as a National Youth Organisation.

The Pony Club is affiliated to British Equestrian.

The Pony Club Office is at **Lowlands Equestrian Centre, Old Warwick Road, Warwick, CV35 7AX,** where The Pony Club is managed by a permanent staff responsible to The Board of Trustees.

THE PONY CLUB LOGO

The logo is a registered Trade Mark and should not be altered in any way without the express permission of The Pony Club. The Pony Club logo should not be incorporated, integrated or positioned so closely to any other logo/s that it appears to be part of that or those logos.

It is very important that, as a Branch or Centre representing The Pony Club, you are using an up to date good resolution logo, in order to show that the Branch / Centre is an official representation of the brand.

Copies of the logo and guidance are available on request to Branches and Centres via The Pony Club website, where you can request the specific type of logo you require.

PONY CLUB COLOURS

Full details of The Pony Club colour palette and how to use them for home and professional printing can be found in the brand guidelines document on The Pony Club website.

PONY CLUB BADGES AND TIES

Members can buy badges and ties from their Branch or Centre or from Pony Club Shop. The official Membership badge should be worn at all Pony Club activities when a jacket is worn. The badge should be worn at Branch / Centre rallies, Shows, Branch or Centre Competitions, Area Competitions and at the Championships.

It should be worn on the left lapel of the jacket. For safety reasons, it must be at least 4cm below the collar bone. A coloured felt showing the highest Test standard achieved by the Member is given to Members by their Branch or Centre. It should be worn behind the Membership badge. Sewn-on badges denoting the Test colours are also available up to B Test for Members wishing to wear them on their sweatshirts or at times when the Members badge is not worn.

Officials' Badges – The officials' badges have the same Pony Club design with a coloured enamel scroll attached bearing the title.

- **Trustee**
  Badge has a chrome surround with blue scroll
- **Area Representative**
  Badge has a chrome surround with a red scroll
- **Sport Chairmen**
  Badge has a chrome surround with blue scroll
- **District Commissioner**
  Badge has a chrome surround with a dark blue scroll
- **Assistant District Commissioner**
  Pale blue scroll
- **Branch Secretary**
  Red scroll
- **Local Committee**
  Dark blue scroll
- **Branch Chief Instructor**
  Green Scroll
- **Instructor's Bar**
  Blue bar bearing the word, Instructor
- **Health & Safety Officer**
  Dark green scroll
- **Treasurer**
  Grey scroll
- **Volunteer**
  White oval

From the point of view of third party insurance, officials are advised to wear the appropriate badge while acting in an official capacity for The Pony Club.

PRESS AND MARKETING

It is in the interests of The Pony Club that its aims and activities are kept in the public eye. Press Releases of Branch and Centre events and invitations can be sent to local press for events. Reports of events should be sent to newspapers immediately after they have taken place. The local BBC and independent radio and television stations are often interested in The Pony Club's activities and you can find templates and information on the officials area of pcuk.org to help you with this type of promotion. If Members are to participate in a radio or television programme, Branches and Centres must inform The Pony Club Office.

MARKETING MATERIALS

The Marketing department can be contacted through The Pony Club Office for any help or advice you may need, and also welcome input into additional resources.

PONY CLUB OFFICIAL CLOTHING

Pony Club clothing is available from **Wainwright Screenprint.**

PONY CLUB PUBLICATIONS

The Pony Club publishes a number of books and e-books on The Pony Club's teaching which are available from Wainwright Screenprint.

HEALTH AND SAFETY AND SAFEGUARDING

Horse Welfare and the Health & Safety of our Members is the absolute top priority for Pony Club UK.

The aim of The Pony Club is to encourage young people to ride and to learn to enjoy all kinds of sport connected with ponies and riding, however by its nature this inevitably involves some risk. Members should be able to learn to ride and participate in equestrian sports in an environment that is as safe and secure as is reasonably practicable. Taking risks, learning the limits and exploring boundaries is a crucial element in a child's development, hence it is imperative that Members are allowed to take risks in a controlled environment to assist their development and to learn how to enjoy equestrian activity safely. The health and safety guidelines are intended to show how organisers, officials and participants can do what is reasonably practicable to ensure the health, safety and welfare of Members and volunteers at Pony Club activities without unnecessarily restricting their enjoyment and learning.

The health & safety requirements of the Pony Club are decided by The Trustees with direction and guidance from the Health and Safety and Welfare Committee. These are published in the Health and Safety Rule Book and Safeguarding Policy (which can be found on the Pony Club website).

The Health and Safety Rulebook includes the following areas:

Risk Assessments

Risk assessment is the cornerstone of good health and safety management and is a vital tool in preventing and/or reducing the risk of injuries. The Pony Club approach to risk assessment is simple, we ask:

- 'How can someone get injured?'; and,
- 'What are we going to do about it?'

Documented risk assessments must be carried out and recorded for all Pony Club activities and events attended by Members.

All areas of a venue/site that everyone has access to should be considered, not just the riding activity or area. Guidelines for the completion of risk assessments and templates are available on the Pony Club website.

Medical and First Aid

A first aider and appointed person must be present at all Pony Club activities. Guidance on the appropriate levels of first aid cover for Pony Club activity and competition can be found in the Health and Safety Rulebook (see First Aid Provision Matrix). The level of medical cover should be considered as part of the risk assessment. Further details can be found in the Health and Safety Rulebook and on The Pony Club website.

Accident Reporting

All injury accidents must be reported using the Risk Reduce online accident reporting website. The full process and link to online Risk Reduce form are available on the health & safety section of the Pony Club website. If in doubt, report it.

Branch Officials' Training (BOT)

What is BOT?

Branch Officials' Training, also referred to as BOT, is a self-guided training package designed to support District Commissioners and branch officials with their roles.

What will you learn?

Through BOT training, you will gain an understanding about:

- · Your role and responsibilities
- · How branches should run in accordance with The Pony Club and charity rules
- · Fundamentals of compliance, including safeguarding, safety, and finance matters
- · Overview of Pony Club coaching and

needs

- · The IT systems available to support with your membership
- · Membership offerings

Who can attend?

Before a new District Commissioner can be ratified in post by the Volunteers and Officials Committee, he/she must complete a BOT Course. It is considered that it would be useful to them for other Branch Officials and Committee members also to undertake the training.

The Volunteers and Officials Committee recommends that District Commissioners (and other Branch Officials) should repeat the training at regular intervals during their time in office.

Insurance

A 'frequently asked questions' information section is available on the Pony Club Website, including all contact details for Howden Insurance.

Horse Welfare

Horse Welfare and the Health & Safety of our Members is the absolute top priority for Pony Club UK. It is our core value that horses and ponies are cared for in the correct environment.

Safeguarding Commitment

The Pony Club believes that it is essential that children and young people are encouraged to take part in outdoor activities and sports as part of their development to adulthood. Their participation in sport must be in a secure, safe and fun environment and be protected from harm. The positive effects of involvement with horses can help develop self-esteem, teamwork and leadership. This can only take place if equestrian sport is effectively regulated and managed by well trained staff and Volunteers.

Safeguarding Policy Statement

The Pony Club has a statutory duty to protect children and safeguard their welfare. Participants in Pony Club activities are entitled to expect a safe and enjoyable environment. The Pony Club policies and procedures are consistent with the British Equestrian (BEF) Safeguarding Policies.

The Safeguarding Policy includes the following areas:

- Duty of care and responsibilities
- How to deal with concerns and allegations
- Safer recruitment practices

Recording Safeguarding Incidents

Any safeguarding incidents/concerns must be logged on the 'MyConcern' portal by the Area Representative or their chosen Area Safeguarding Lead.

INSURANCE

The Pony Club has a comprehensive portfolio of insurance, designed to give protection to the Association and its Members (including Centre Members), Branches, Volunteers and Employees. The insurances are arranged by The Pony Club's broker – Howden, One Creechurch Place, London, EC3A 5AF Tel: 020 7645 9339. Amongst the most important policies are the liability policies. It should be noted that the liability insurances deal with claims made against The Pony Club or Members on a legal liability basis and not a moral liability basis.

The Pony Club Public Liability Insurance

This policy covers claims made against The Pony Club or a Pony Club Branch (based in Great Britain and Northern Ireland) or a person acting on their behalf arising out of the usual activities of The Pony Club or a Branch anywhere in the world. It covers accidental bodily injury to members of the public or damage to their property as a result of negligence. The limit of indemnity is thirty million pounds (£30M) in respect of any one occurrence.

Only normal Pony Club activities are automatically included – if a Branch wishes to engage in an activity outside of the normal activities for a Branch they should notify The Pony Club Office who will consult with insurers if necessary.

If a Branch is asked to provide an indemnity (perhaps by the owner of land that will be used by the Branch for an activity), the wording of any such indemnity must be referred to The Pony Club, Lowlands Equestrian Centre, Old Warwick Road, Warwick, CV35 7AX Tel: 02476 698300. Email: enquiries@pcuk.org: for approval before it is signed by the District Commissioner.

This policy will deal only with claims made against The Pony Club or Branches by third parties and will not cover damage to property belonging to The Pony Club or a Pony Club Branch or property in their care, custody or control. If cover is required for damage to property you should arrange separate insurance.

The Pony Club Employers' Liability Insurance

This policy covers claims made by employees against The Pony Club or Branch (based in Great Britain or Northern Ireland) arising out of the usual activities of The Pony Club or Branch anywhere in Great Britain, Northern Ireland, the Channel Islands or the Isle of Man (extended to world-wide for temporary visits by employees). It covers accidental bodily injury to any employee including any casual labourer such as a coach. The limit of indemnity is ten million pounds (£10M) in respect of any one occurrence but five million pounds (£5M) for terrorism or asbestos claims.

The Pony Club Members' Personal Liability Insurance

This policy covers claims made against the Member for accidental bodily injury to members of the public or damage to their property arising out of the Member's use or ownership or control of a horse or pony or horse/pony-drawn vehicle at any time – not just at Pony Club activities. Also covered are other persons using the Member's horse or pony or horse/pony-drawn vehicle with the Member's permission, unless such person is insured elsewhere. Cover is restricted to accidents occurring within the United Kingdom or Republic of Ireland

The Member's liability policy is one of 'last resort'. Therefore if any other policy is in place which would cover the claim, the alternative policy will respond before The Pony Club policy. Many household or equine mortality policies will include public liability cover and this will be explored before a claim is accepted under The Pony Club policy.

If the Member is a child and is too young to be found legally liable, then the policy will cover the parent or guardian of the Member for liability arising out of the Member's activities as provided for in the policy. Temporary Members are covered whilst attending Pony Club activities (from time of arrival until time of departure) only if they are attending a rally with a view to joining The Pony Club. This applies to a couple of rallies only.

The limit of indemnity is thirty million pounds

(£30M) in respect of any one occurrence.

The policy does not cover:

- accidental bodily injury to the Member or anyone in the Member's family, household or employ or damage to any such person's property or property in their care, custody or control.
- accidents occurring whilst the Member is engaged in racing, point to point, steeplechasing, team chasing or any other form of racing other than Endurance Riding or Official Pony Club Race Days and Training Days.
- accidents arising out of any business activities or the use of the Member's horse or pony or horse/pony-drawn vehicle for hire and reward.
- The first £250 of any claim for property damage.

For any queries relating to Pony Club insurance please contact:
Catherine Morgan
Catherine.morgan@howdengroup.com
Tel: 020 7645 9339

An Insurance Product Information Document and the policy wording for The Pony Club Members cover can be printed from pcuk.org under Join Us > Parents Information > Members Insurance

MEMBERSHIP

Branch Membership

Subscriptions (See Rule 8 For Definitions)

	Individual Member	Family Membership (as defined in rule 8.6)	Non-Riding Member
Full Year	**£86**	**£212**	**£41**
Branch Revenue Share	**£21**	**£53**	**£10**

Late Submission Fees

Branches incurring late submission fees as specified in Rule 21.12 will be charged at the following rates:

- Overdue: £2.00 per Member
- One month overdue: an additional £3.00 per Member

The Membership shall be calculated on the reported Membership of the Branch for the preceding Pony Club year.

Appeals

In accordance with Rule 20.4 of The Pony Club, the deposit required to lodge an appeal will be £100.00.

Forming a New Branch

Any person wishing to form a new Branch should consult the Area Representative for advice and guidance.

Centre Membership

	Centre Member	Centre Plus Member
Full Year	**£41**	**£86**
Centre Revenue Share Incentive	**£5**	**£10**

COACHES AND TRAINING

The Pony Club aims to offer the best possible coaching and opportunities to its members at all levels.

Learning about the care and welfare of horses and ponies is paramount to Pony Club ethos. Through working rallies, training, and camps our members can progress in their riding and care knowledge using our achievement badges and tests to help them develop their skills.

Having a Pony Club rally organiser or lead coach is strongly recommended, they will work alongside the District Commissioner. The District Commissioner should always be available to answer queries and discuss problems which may arise. The lead coach must have attended a Pony Club Continuing Professional Development (CPD) course. The lead coach may be a member of the Branch / Centre Committee, and is responsible for:

- Arranging the instructional programme for rallies and camp (using the **Pony Club Training Pathway** is recommended).
- Ensuring that facilities are risk assessed before use and that the equipment is ready for each rally/camp.
- Approve coaches for rallies and be able to brief the coach accordingly.
- Finding coaches with specialised knowledge.
- Organising meetings and practical sessions for coaches and ensure that all coach requirements are up to date.
- Advising coaches on suitable CPD courses.
- Organise any relevant training relating to Branch or Centre team selection.
- Assist in the preparation of members wishing to take their Pony Club tests.

Coaches' Courses

The Pony Club believes that part of its mission is to train its own future coaches. Potential coaches come from all age groups but particularly from older members who have had the benefit of being part of The Pony Club community. The Training Committee recommends a specific route for new coaches without a formal equestrian coaching qualification which is the Introduction to Pony Club Coaching Steps 1-3 Courses.

For a course to count as a CPD course, it must be notified to The Pony Club Office, for inclusion on the website at least one week in advance of the course date. Courses may be run by any Branch, Centre, or Area, with the approval of the Area Representative. Guidance on what courses to offer can be found on The Pony Club website.

The Pony Club Manual of Horsemanship

The Manual is a complete basic guide to horsemanship and riding. Currently in its updated 14th edition it is a worldwide bestseller, containing information on a wide range of equestrian topics. The manual should be used as the basis for all instruction to members.

Coaching

One of the objectives of The Pony Club is to offer instruction and coaching sessions which enable members to develop both their riding and understanding of equine care. Coaches must base their teaching on The Pony Club Manual of Horsemanship to avoid conflicting methods.

Pony Club coaches are divided into categories according to their use and role within The Pony Club. It is a requirement that all coaches used by The Pony Club are listed as active coaches on PELHAM. Further information can be found on The Pony Club website. Coaches without an up to date Enhanced DBS or Safeguarding certificate must not be used.

The Pony Club Tests

Test Fees

Tests E, D, D+, Road Rider, C, C+ are organised at Branch/Centre level and do not attract standard fees.

B, B+, Lungeing, and AH tests are organised at Area level.

A tests are organised by The Pony Club Office

Charges to cover venues and Assessors' expenses etc. may be levied at the District Commissioner's, Centre Proprietor's or Area Representative's discretion.

Current Test Fees

B Test	**£60 per section**
B+ Test	**£95**
Lungeing Test	**£45**
AH Test	**£180 full test (8 sections)** **£140 (4 sections)** **£45 per section**
A Test	**£240 full test**

Assessor Fees

B Test	**£145 full day** **£80 half day**
B+ Test	**£145 per test** **(if second test on the same day + £70)**
Lungeing Test	**£35 per candidate (no more than £170 for a full day)**
AH Test	**£180 full day** **£100 half day**
A Test	**£225**

For tests below B Test, the fees may vary, but should not exceed the B Test Assessor Fees for a full or half day.

Test Colours

A coloured disc or felt (obtainable by Branches and Centres from The Pony Club Shop) will be issued to members to denote the test standard achieved. The disc or felt representing the highest test achieved by the Member should be worn behind the membership badge. Successful candidates are also awarded a certificate in the appropriate colour.

The colours should be awarded as follows: -

- E – Pale Yellow
- D - Yellow
- D+ - White
- C (Horse & Pony Care) - Meadow Green
- C (Riding) - Silver Grey
- C both sections - Green
- C+ (Horse & Pony Care) - Turquoise
- C+ (Riding) - Burgundy
- C+ both sections - Pink
- B (Riding) - Beige
- B (Horse & Pony Care) - Brown
- B both sections - Red
- Lungeing test - Light Blue
- B+ - Pale Purple
- AH - Orange
- AH with Distinction - Orange
- AH with Honours - Salmon Pink
- A - Blue
- A with Distinction - Blue

A with Honours - Purple

Reasonable Adjustments

The Pony Club is committed to ensuring that, wherever possible, members are able to access all aspects of the Branch and Centre activities we offer. Reasonable Adjustments are any actions that help to reduce the effect of a disability or difficulty. They are needed because some disabilities can make it harder for members to take part in activities than it would have been had the member not been disabled. A Member does not necessarily have to be disabled (as defined by the Equality Act 2010) to be allowed an access arrangement. Reasonable Adjustments are intended to increase access to Tests and other activities and are intended to assist Members in demonstrating their attainment without affecting or circumventing the Test requirements. All Reasonable Adjustment Plans will be treated confidentially and only shared with permission from the member and their parent (if under 18yrs old).

Reasonable Adjustments can be used for the Pony Club Tests and should be approved in advance of the Test taking place. Reasonable Adjustments are changes made to an assessment or to the way an assessment is conducted that reduce or remove a disadvantage caused by a student's disability. Reasonable Adjustments will not affect the reliability or validity of the Test outcome nor should they give the Member an assessment advantage over other Members undertaking the same or similar Tests. Where possible the Reasonable Adjustment should reflect a Member's normal way of working. The Reasonable Adjustment is intended to give all Pony Club Members a level playing field in which to demonstrate their skills, knowledge and understanding.

Reasonable Adjustments can also be used to allow for members to take part in activities or competitions. As with Tests these adjustments should be approved in advance of the activity or competition. For more information, please refer to the Reasonable Adjustment Policy which can be found on the website.

Some Pony Club members may already have an Education, Health and Care Plan (EHCP) which can be used to help plan Reasonable Adjustments. However, the Pony Club will strive to ensure inclusivity for any of its members who need additional support whether or not they have an official statement.

PONY CLUB ACTIVITIES

WORKING RALLIES

The working rally continues to be an important part of Pony Club training with the main objectives being to encourage and improve members' riding skills and their knowledge of equine care and management.

Rallies must be advertised at least seven days prior to the date of the rally and organised by Branch / Centre Committees. Nobody can hold a rally or coach at a rally unless authorised by the District Commissioner, Branch Committee or Centre Proprietor.

A working rally is one at which coaching is given and which is open to all members of the Branch / Centre within the age range or ability level for which it is intended, it may be mounted or dismounted. A dismounted rally is usually used for horse and pony care instruction.

The Pony Club syllabus of coaching in The Pony Club Instructors' Handbook offers guidance on how to build a programme. The timetable and the coaching given at Rallies should be carefully planned.

UNSUITABLE HORSES/PONIES AND UNSUITABLE SADDLERY

Members may come to mounted rallies on horses/ponies which are unsuitable for them or with ill-fitting saddlery that is unserviceable. This can make instruction difficult and the safety of both rider and horse/pony must take precedence. Members coming to a rally for the first time who may not know of The Pony Club's standards and training ethos which will need addressing with tact and sympathy and offered in the form of education and encouragement.

At the start of every working rally the coach should observe riders to ensure the correct gear is worn, and check on the fitting of tack, giving appropriate advice. Where there is a problem, which makes riding impossible, or dangerous, the rider should be asked to dismount and the problem passed to The Pony Club official in charge of the rally. If there is need to involve the member's parents this should be done by the District Commissioner/ Centre Proprietor or the Rally Organiser. Action by the coach is not recommended.

COMPETITIONS

Open Horse Shows and Competitions

To raise funds some Branches and Centres organise shows or competitions that are open to non- Members.

A disclaimer should be included in the programme for all shows and competitions organised by Branches/Centres. The suggested wording is:

"Legal Liability: Save for the death or personal injury caused by the negligence of the organisers, or anyone for whom they are in law responsible, neither the organisers of this event or The Pony Club nor any agent, employee or representative of these bodies, nor the landlord or his tenant, accepts any liability for any accident, loss, damage, injury or illness to horses, owners, riders, spectators, land, cars, their contents and accessories, or any other person or property whatsoever. Entries are only accepted on this basis.

Health & Safety: Organisers of this event have taken reasonable precautions to ensure the health and safety of everyone present. For these measures to be effective, everyone must take all reasonable precautions to avoid and prevent accidents occurring and must obey the instructions of the organisers and all the officials and stewards.

Competitors who are not members of The Pony Club are not covered by The Pony Club insurance and must have their own third party cover. The [XX] Branch of The Pony Club/[xx} Pony Club Centre and the organisers of this event are not legally responsible for non-Members and their insurance will not cover you."

When holding classes for which conditions have been laid down, and judges appointed by a governing body, Branches and Centres are recommended to seek advice from the organisation concerned.

Prizes

It is against Pony Club policy to encourage children to be 'pot hunters' and money prizes are forbidden at competitions or shows for Pony Club Members only.

Competitions Open to Members of other Branches or Centres

Members and organisers of events must follow the Rule for Competitions organised by Branches and Centres.

If an event is open to competitors from other Branches or Centres, it is important to put in the schedule under which Rules it is run and any local modifications.

Types Of Competition

Dismounted

- National Quiz
- Horse & Pony Care Competition
- Triathlon
- Art Competition

Mounted

- Dressage
- Dressage to Music
- Endurance
- Equitation Dressage and Show Jumping
- Eventing (including Arena Eventing)
- Hunter Trials
- Mounted Games
- Musical Ride
- Pony Racing
- Polo
- Polocrosse
- Show Jumping
- Tetrathlon

HUNTING

The Pony Club and its Branches are entirely separate organisations to any hunts. Historically Branches were founded by members of local Hunts for the benefit of their farmers' and subscribers' children.

The Pony Club recognises that hunting has changed following the inception of the Hunting Act 2004 on 18th February 2005. As long as hunts are acting within the law, The Pony Club continues to encourage those Members who wish to take part and experience riding across country to do so.

Trail-hunting, hound exercise and exempt hunting are recognised activities that hunts participate in to comply with the current legislation.

EXCHANGES BETWEEN BRANCHES, CENTRES AND INTERNATIONAL VISITS

The Pony Club believes that visits and the exchange of ideas between Branches and Centres offers a great benefit to Members. The sharing of interests with Members from different Branches and Centres and from different countries broadens a Member's experience.

Areas, Branches or Centres wanting to arrange exchanges or visits, where they will be representing The Pony Club, with countries or overseas Branches or Centres must first get permission from The Pony Club Office and their Area Representative. Details of these visits must be sent to The Pony Club Office and their Area Representative who will give guidance and support where possible. At the end of any visit, a written report will be required by The Pony Club Office.

For an exchange that relates to a specific sport please take note of the selection criteria which apply to that sport, available on The Pony Club website.

All International invitations are made direct to The Pony Club Office in conjunction with the Pony Club International Alliance (PCIA).

YOUTH PROGRAMMES

Young Equestrian Leader Award (YELA)

The Young Equestrian Leaders Award is a scheme which recognises the time and effort that young people put in to volunteering in equestrian sport. It is open to Pony Club Members aged between 13 and 25 with three levels available: Bronze, Silver and Gold. The progressive requirements at each level encourage young people to develop a range of skills, gain experiences and learn more about the industry in view of shaping them to become leaders of the future.

Once registered, young people will be sent a log book to track and record their volunteering, with just 20 hours gaining them the Bronze level. For more information please visit The Pony Club website or email yela@pcuk.org

THE PONY CLUB WEBSITE

Aim

The purpose of The Pony Club Website is to provide a source of information, education and interactive activities for all. It can be found at pcuk.org.

The Branch And Area Sites

All Branches and Areas have their own sub-site which can be accessed and updated. These websites can be found through the "Find a Club" listings on pcuk.org

The District Commissioner should call for a volunteer to take on the responsibility of acting as Web Manager and managing the Branch site. Each Branch is responsible for writing and updating its own Branch pages and must have access to a computer, which can connect to the Internet, in order to do this. Each site can have multiple managers if required. The Pony Club will never ask you for your password.

THE PONY CLUB EMAIL SYSTEM

All Branches and Areas have their own email address ending in @pcuk.org to which all official communications will be sent, at least one member of the Branch committee must have access to this email account.
The District Commissioner/Treasurer must regularly monitor the DC.Branch@pcuk.org /Treasurer.Branch@pcuk.org email accounts to ensure emails of a sensitive nature remain confidential. Emails can be accessed through a webmail interface, by using software such as Microsoft Outlook or by adding to a phone or tablet. Access details and further information can be requested by contacting The Pony Club Office or the PELHAM Support hub: https://pelham.pcuk.org/The Pelham System

This system keeps a list of all current and past Members for each Branch or Centre along with information on Branch/Centre Officials and Coaches. All new Members and renewing Members are processed via the online, self-service Member Portal or The Pony Club Office for both Branch and Centres.

All Branches are required to keep the contact information up-to-date on a regular basis to satisfy both insurance requirements and Data Protection legislation. Branches MUST also record Tests and Achievement Badges on this system.

Branches must maintain up-to-date coach information, including Disclosure, Safeguarding, First Aid and CPD certifications on PELHAM.

Centres - please regularly check your Membership records. Centres MUST also record Tests and Achievement Badges on this system. Coach data for Centres will be updated by Centre Co-ordinators or The Pony Club Office.

In addition to holding data, the PELHAM system provides email facility for Branches to use to contact their Members and coaches and facilitates transfer of Members.

Branches must update their rallies and events into Pelham, either via the manual function or via one of the entry systems licensed to integrate with Pelham which provide membership validation. A list of these licensed partners is available on the pcuk.org website

You do not require any special software to access PELHAM; you just need a computer with internet access. Please check the PELHAM support site for user guides and up- to-date information: https://pelham.pcuk.org

TRAVELLING EXPENSES

In accordance with Rule 12.5, the currently approved rate when travelling by car is 45 pence per mile for the first 10,000 miles, and 25 pence per mile for any subsequent mileage.

Pony Club Areas

AREA 1

Area Representative: Sue Cheape

area1@pcuk.org
07974 692535

Centre Coordinator: Adrian Macleod

area1.centres@pcuk.org
07866 631875

BRANCHES

- Angus
- Bennachie
- Caithness
- Deeside
- Deveron
- East Aberdeenshire (Buchan)
- East Stirlingshire
- Fife Hunt
- Forth Valley
- Glenrothes
- Inverness-shire
- Kincardineshire
- Moray & Nairn
- North Argyll
- Orkney
- Perth Hunt
- Ross-shire
- Strathearn
- West Perthshire
- Western Isles

CENTRES

- Broomhill Riding Centre
- Castle View Stables
- Dark Deer Croft
- Glen Tanar Equestrian Centre
- Gleneagles Equestrian Centre
- Hayfield EC
- NMW Riding Academy
- Pathhead Equestrian Centre
- Scholland Equestrian at Kilconquhar
- Skye Trekking Centre
- The Leys Riding School (prev. Sea Horse Stables)
- Wardhaugh Farm
- Wester Dowald Equine Centre

AREA 2

Area Representative: Michelle Macaulay

area2@pcuk.org
07765 925850

Centre Coordinator: Sarah Lewins

area2.centres@pcuk.org
07799 404246

BRANCHES

- Braes of Derwent South
- Cleveland Hunt
- Cumberland Farmers' Hunt (South)
- Cumberland Farmers Hunt North
- Cumberland Foxhounds
- Morpeth Hunt
- Newcastle & North Durham
- North Northumberland Hunt
- Percy Hunt
- South Durham Hunt
- South Northumberland
- Tynedale Hunt
- Wyndham
- Zetland Hunt

CENTRES

- Eston Equitation Centre
- Field House Equestrian Centre
- Finchale View Riding School
- Murton Equestrian Centre
- Robinsons Equiteach
- Rookin House Farm

AREA 3

Area Representative: Nicky Morrison

area3@pcuk.org
07850 617245

Centre Coordinator: John Gilbert

area3.centres@pcuk.org
07837 597561

BRANCHES

- Badsworth Hunt

- Bedale & West of Yore Hunt
- Bramham Moor Hunt
- Derwent Hunt
- Glaisdale Hunt
- Holderness Hunt
- Hurworth Hunt
- Middleton Hunt
- Middleton Hunt (East Side)
- Rockwood Harriers
- Ryburn Valley
- Sinnington Hunt
- Staintondale Hunt
- Vale of York
- York & Ainsty North
- York & Ainsty South

CENTRES

- Angel Riding Centre
- Batley Hall Farm Riding Centre
- Bewerley Riding Centre
- Bridge End Equestrian
- Burnby Equestrian Centre
- Cliffhollins Riding School
- Friars Hill Stables
- Grenoside Equestrian Centre Ltd
- Lacys Cottage Riding School
- Lime Oaks Equestrian Centre
- Naburn Grange Riding Centre
- Oxmardyke Equestrian Centre
- Riverside Equestrian Centre
- Throstle Nest Riding School
- Tong Lane End Equestrian Centre
- Willerby Hill Riding School

AREA 4

Area Representative: Robin Bower
area4@pcuk.org
07976 272272

Centre Coordinator: John Gilbert
area4.centres@pcuk.org
07837 597561

BRANCHES

- Blackburn & District
- Chipping
- Furness & District
- Fylde & District
- Glossop & District
- Haydock Park
- Holcombe Hunt
- Isle of Man
- Lancaster & District
- Oxenholme
- Peak
- Pendle Forest & Craven Hunt
- Saddleworth & District
- West Lancashire County
- West Lancashire Ince Blundell
- Wheelton & District

CENTRES

- Accrington Riding Centre
- Ballawhetstone
- Beaumont Grange Farm
- Bigland Hall Equine Group
- Bowlers Riding School
- Burrows Lane Farm Riding School
- Casterton Sedbergh Prep School
- Croft Riding Centre Pony Club
- Darlington Stables
- Deandane Riding Stables
- Eccleston Equestrian Centre
- Holt's Equestrian Centre
- Kilnsey Trekking and Riding Centre
- Landlords Farm Equestrian Centre
- Larkrigg Riding School
- Lodge Riding Centre
- Longfield Equestrian Centre
- Midgeland Riding School
- Moorview Equestrian Centre
- New Hill House
- Park Palace Ponies
- Robin House Equestrian
- Roocroft Riding Stables
- Seaview Riding School
- Witherslack Hall Equestrian Centre
- Wrea Green Equitation Centre

AREA 5

Area Representative: Susan Goodridge
area5@pcuk.org
07765 327126

Centre Coordinator: John Gilbert
area5.centres@pcuk.org
07837 597561

BRANCHES

- Aberconwy
- Anglesey
- Berwyn & Dee
- Burton Cheshire Forest Hunt
- Cheshire Hunt North
- Cheshire Hunt South
- Dolgellau & District
- Dwyfor
- East Cheshire
- Flint & Denbigh Hunt
- Gwynedd
- Sir W W Wynn's Hunt
- Tanatside Hunt
- Waen-y-Llyn

CENTRES

- Anglesey Riding Centre
- Bridlewood Riding Centre
- Cheshire Riding School
- Conwy Community Riding Centre
- Oakhanger Riding and Pony Club Centre
- Pen Y Coed Riding Stables
- Springbank Riding School
- Wirral Riding Centre

AREA 6

Area Representative: Patrick Campbell
area6@pcuk.org
07801 423898

Centre Coordinator: Amelia Morris-Payne
area6.centres@pcuk.org
07816 955757

BRANCHES

- Barlow Hunt
- Belvoir Hunt
- Blankney Hunt
- Brocklesby Hunt
- Burghley
- Burton Hunt
- Cottesmore Hunt
- Fernie Hunt
- Fitzwilliam Hunt
- Grove Hunt
- High Peak Hunt
- Meynell Hunt
- Quorn Hunt
- Rufford Hunt
- Scunthorpe & District
- South Nottinghamshire
- South Trent
- South Wold Hunt North
- Woodland Pytchley Hunt

CENTRES

- Almond Equestrian
- Bulby Hall Equestrian Centre
- Chestnut Farm Stables
- Coloured Cob Equestrian Centre
- Cottagers Plot Equestrian Centre
- Dovecote Farm Equestrian Centre
- Folly Farm Equestrian Centre
- Glapthorn Manor Equestrian
- Grove House Stables Pony Club Centre
- Hargate Equestrian
- Hundleby Riding Centre
- Langtoft Stables
- Long Lane Equestrian
- Mill House
- New Direction
- Newark Equestrian
- Oakfield Farm Pony Club Centre
- Oldmoor Farm Riding School
- P and R Equestrian Centre
- Parklands Arena
- Parkside Stables
- Parkview Riding School
- Red Piece Equestrian Stables
- Snowdon Farm Riding School
- Somerby Equestrian Centre
- Southview Equestrian Centre

Stickney Riding Centre

AREA 7

Area Representative: Andrew James
area7@pcuk.org
01455 291273 / 07737 877697

Centre Coordinator: Amelia Morris-Payne
area7.centres@pcuk.org
07816 955757

BRANCHES

- Albrighton Hunt
- Albrighton Woodland Hunt
- Atherstone Hunt
- Heart of England
- Ludlow Hunt
- North Shropshire Hunt
- North Staffordshire Hunt
- North Warwickshire
- Pytchley Hunt
- South Shropshire Hunt
- South Staffordshire Hunt
- United Pack
- Warwickshire Hunt
- West Midlands
- West Warwickshire
- Wheatland Hunt

CENTRES

- Appletree Stud
- Beaver Hall
- Bishton Hall Riding School
- Bourne Vale Riding Stables
- Brampton Stables
- Corner Farm Equestrian
- Coton House Farm Stables
- Courses for Horses
- Coventry and District Pony Club
- East Lodge Farm Equestrian Centre
- Equine Learning
- Featherbed Stables
- Foxhills Riding Centre
- Grafton Farm Riding Centre Ltd
- Hole Farm Trekking Centre
- K A Horses
- Lodge Farm Equestrian Centre
- Lychgate Farm Equestrian LLP
- Moor Farm Stables
- NTC Pony Club
- Nuneaton and North Warwickshire Equestrian Centre
- Offchurch Bury Polo Club
- Radway Equestrian
- Rockstar Equine
- Rookery Team Pony Club
- Stourport Riding Centre
- Summerfield Stables
- Valley Farm Equestrian Centre Ltd
- Witham Villa Riding Centre
- Woodbine Stables

AREA 8

Area Representative: Hetta Wilkinson
area8@pcuk.org
07880 728708 / 01206 330476

Centre Coordinator: Di Pegrum
area8.centres@pcuk.org
07890 919558

BRANCHES

- Cambridgeshire Hunt
- East Essex Hunt
- Easton Harriers Hunt
- Enfield Chace Hunt
- Essex & Suffolk Hunt
- Essex Farmers
- Essex Hunt North
- Essex Union
- Essex Union South
- Littleport & District
- Newmarket & Thurlow Hunt
- North Norfolk
- Puckeridge Hunt
- Puckeridge Hunt Western
- Soham & District
- South Norfolk
- Suffolk Hunt
- Thetford Chase
- Walpole & District
- Waveney Harriers

- West Norfolk Hunt

CENTRES

- Aldborough Hall Equestrian Centre
- Annabelles Equestrian
- Apollo Stables
- Barnfields Chingford Riding School
- Brook Cottage Farm Riding School
- Deanswood Equestrian Centre
- Fletchers Farm Riding School
- Gillians Riding School Pony Club Centre
- Gym-Khana
- Hall Farm Stables
- Hertfordshire Polo Academy (Moor Hall/ Silverleys)
- Hill Farm Equestrian Centre (8)
- Hill Farm Stables (Elmswell)
- Hilltop Equestrian Centre
- Hooks Cross Equestrian
- Hot to Trot School of Equitation
- Iken Bay Riding
- Kimblewick Equestrian Centre
- Lee Valley Riding Centre
- Little Wratting Riding School
- Moat Farm Riding Centre
- Park Hall Equestrian
- Petasfield Stables
- Roman Bank Equestrian
- Sawston Riding School
- The British Racing School
- Trent Park Equestrian Centre
- Willow Farm Riding School
- Old Tiger Stables at North Angle Farm

AREA 9

Area Representative: Pleasance Jewitt
area9@pcuk.org
01285 821715

Centre Coordinator: Emma Stoba
area9.centres@pcuk.org
07792 839921

BRANCHES

- Beaufort Hunt
- Berkeley Hunt
- Berkeley Hunt South
- Cotswold Hunt
- Cotswold Vale Farmers' Hunt
- Croome Hunt
- Heythrop Hunt
- Ledbury Hunt
- Malvern
- Minchinhampton
- North Cotswold Hunt
- North Herefordshire Hunt
- Old Berkshire Hunt
- South Hereford and Ross Harriers
- Stroud
- VWH Hunt
- Worcestershire Hunt
- Wyre Forest

CENTRES

- Asti Equestrian
- Bourton Vale Equestrian Centre
- Cotswold Polo Academy
- Cotswold Riding
- Foxcote House Riding School
- Huntersfield Equestrian Centre
- Noakes Farm Riding Centre
- Pigeon House Equestrian
- Putley Pony Club Centre
- Regal Equestrian
- Shrivenham Equestrian Centre
- St James City Farm and Riding School
- Tewkesbury Pony Club Centre
- The Elms
- The Talland School of Equitation
- Tipton Hall Riding School
- Tumpy Green Equestrian & Competition Centre
- Wickstead Farm Equestrian Centre
- Worcester Riding School and Pony Club Centre

AREA 10

Area Representative: Isobel Mills
area10@pcuk.org
07976 779140

Centre Coordinator: Emma Coates
area10.centres@pcuk.org
07973 677820

BRANCHES

- Brecon & Talybont Hunt
- Crickhowell & District
- Curre Hunt
- Dare Valley
- Dinas Powys
- Glamorgan Hunt
- Golden Valley Hunt
- Irfon & Tywi
- Kenfig Hill
- Llangeinor Hunt
- Monmouthshire
- Pentyrch
- Radnor & West Hereford Hunt
- Sennybridge & District
- Teme Valley Hunt
- Tredegar Farmers Hunt
- Ynysybwl

- **CENTRES**
- Cantref Pony Club Centre
- Cardiff Riding School
- Green Meadow Riding Centre
- Liege Manor Equestrian
- Lucton School
- Severnvale Equestrian Centre
- Smugglers Equestrian Centre
- Sunnybank Equestrian Centre
- Talygarn Equestrian Centre
- Tregoyd Riding Centre
- Triley Fields Equestrian Centre
- Underhill Riding Stables

AREA 11

Area Representative: Abby Bernard
area11@pcuk.org
07775 712512

Centre Coordinator: Sarah Glynn-Brooks
area11.centres@pcuk.org
07816 784487

BRANCHES

- Ashford Valley
- Cobham and Wimbledon
- Crawley & Horsham Hunt
- East Kent Hunt
- East Sussex
- Eridge Hunt
- Kent Border
- Mid Surrey
- Old Surrey & Burstow Hunt
- Romney Marsh
- Southdown Hunt (East)
- Southdown Hunt West
- Surrey Union
- Tickham Hunt
- West Kent (Sevenoaks)
- West Kent Meopham

CENTRES

- Barton Field Farm Equestrian Centre
- Bradbourne Riding and Training Centre
- Buckswood School Stables
- Bursted Hill Stables
- Cornilo Riding
- Deepdene Riding Stables
- Ebony Horse Club
- Ghyll Park Equestrian
- Grassroots
- Grove Farm Riding School
- Hemsted Forest Equestrian Centre
- Kingsmead Equestrian Centre
- Little Brook Equestrian
- Mannix Equestrian Centre
- Mierscourt Valley Riding School
- Mount Mascal Stables
- Nelson Park Riding Centre
- Old Bexley Stables Pony Club
- Park Farm Riding School
- Park Lane Stables
- Pine Ridge Riding School
- Quarry Farm Riding Stables
- Ridge Farm Riding School
- Royal Alexandra and Albert School RS
- Rye Street Farm Equestrian Centre
- Saddles Riding Centre
- South Farm Riding Stables

- Southborough Lane Stables
- Squirrells Riding School
- St Teresa's Equestrian
- Stag Lodge
- Tandridge Priory Riding Centre
- The 4 Gaits Riding School
- The Owl House Stables
- The Stables at Cissbury
- Timbertops Equestrian Centre
- Valley Riding School
- Wellgrove Farm Equestrian
- Whiteleaf Riding Stables
- Wildwoods Riding Centre

AREA 12

Area Representative: Helen Jackson
area12@pcuk.org
01494 881321 / 07941 818738

Centre Coordinator: Di Pegrum
area12.centres@pcuk.org
07890 919558

BRANCHES

- Bedfordshire South
- Bicester & Warden Hill Hunt
- East Hertfordshire Hunt
- Flamstead
- Grafton Hunt
- Hertfordshire Hunt
- Ivel Valley
- Oakley Hunt North
- Oakley Hunt West
- Old Berkeley Hunt (Chilterns)
- Old Berkeley Hunt (Hughenden)
- Old Berkeley Hunt (North)
- Old Berkeley Hunt (South)
- South Hertfordshire
- South Oxfordshire Hunt (South)
- South Oxfordshire Hunt Central
- Vale of Aylesbury Hunt
- Whaddon Chase
- Woodland Hunt
- Wormwood Scrubs

CENTRES

- Baylands Equestrian Centre
- Blisworth Pony Club Centre
- Ealing Riding School
- Echos Equestrian
- Evergreen Stables
- Littlebourne Equestrian Centre
- Oxford Polo
- Sandridgebury Riding School
- Shardeloes Farm Equestrian Centre
- Silverstone Riding Stables
- Waterstock Dressage Ltd
- Widmer Equestrian

AREA 13

Area Representative: Andrea Hurley
area13@pcuk.org
07967 683207

Centre Coordinator: Sally Blackmore
area13.centres@pcuk.org
07442 530080

BRANCHES

- Bisley and Sandown Chase
- Chiddingfold
- Chiddingfold Farmers
- Cowdray Hunt
- Crawley & Horsham Hunt South
- Garth Hunt
- Garth South
- Goodwood
- Hambledon Hunt (North)
- Hampshire Hunt
- Isle of Wight
- Lord Leconfield Hunt
- Petersfield
- South Berkshire
- Staff College & Sandhurst
- Vine
- Wokingham

CENTRES

- Badshot Lea Equestrian Centre
- Barnfield Riding School
- Berkshire Riding Centre

- Broadlands Riding Centre
- Cool Hooves Polo
- Cranleigh School Equestrian Centre
- Equestrian at Coworth Park
- Fort Widley Equestrian Centre
- Gleneagles Equestrian Centre (Area 13)
- Greatham Equestrian Centre
- Greenways Stables Ltd
- Hewshott Farm Stables
- Hill Farm Riding Stables and Pony Club Centre (IoW)
- Inadown Farm Livery Stables
- Island Riding Centre
- Kiln Stables Riding School
- Lands End Equestrian Centre
- Northington Stud and Stables
- Pony Grove
- Russells Equestrian Centre
- Shedfield Equestrian Centre
- Silvermere Equestrian Centre
- Wellington Riding

AREA 14

Area Representative: Louly Thornycroft
area14@pcuk.org
01258 860614

Centre Coordinator: Jacqui Bolt
area14.centres@pcuk.org
07790 970048

BRANCHES

- Avon Vale Hunt
- Banwell
- Blackmore & Sparkford Vale Hunt
- Cattistock Hunt
- Craven Hunt
- Guernsey
- Hursley Hunt
- Jersey Drag Hunt
- Mendip Farmers' Hunt
- New Forest Hunts
- Poole & District
- Portman Hunt
- Royal Artillery
- South & West Wilts Hunt
- South Dorset Hunt
- Syston
- Tedworth Hunt
- West Hants
- Wilton Hunt
- Wylye Valley

CENTRES

- Alstone Court Riding Establishment
- Burley Villa School of Riding
- Church Farm Equestrian Centre
- Dorset Polo Club
- Hanford School
- Knighton House School
- Otterbourne Riding Centre
- Pevlings Farm Riding and Livery Stables
- Rosewall Equestrian
- Royal Armoured Corps Saddle Club
- Sandroyd School
- SMS Equestrian
- Stonar School Equestrian Centre
- Tedworth Equestrian
- Wick Riding School
- Widbrook Arabian Stud and Equestrian Centre

AREA 15

Area Representative: Deborah Custance–Baker
area15@pcuk.org
01392 861750 / 07889 260446

Centre Coordinator: Jacqui Bolt
area15.centres@pcuk.org
07790 970078

BRANCHES

- Axe Vale Hunt
- Cotley Hunt
- Devon & Somerset
- Dulverton West Foxhounds (North Molton) Hunt
- East Devon Hunt
- Polden Hills
- Quantock Hunt

- Seavington
- Silverton Hunt
- Taunton Vale
- Taunton Vale Harriers
- Tiverton Hunt
- West Somerset
- Weston Harriers Hunt

CENTRES

- Bowdens Riding School at Balham
- Comeytrowe Equestrian Centre
- Currypool Equestrian
- Mutterton Equine
- Oaklands Riding School (Area 15)
- Red Park Equestrian Centre

AREA 16

Area Representative: Karen Harris
area16@pcuk.org
07470 366000

Centre Coordinator: Helen Moore
area16.centres@pcuk.org
07828 837784

BRANCHES

- Cury Hunt
- Dartmoor Hunt
- East Cornwall Hunt
- Eggesford Hunt
- Four Burrow Hunt
- Lamerton Hunt
- Mid Devon Hunt
- North Cornwall
- South Devon Hunt (Moorland)
- South Devon West
- South Pool
- Spooners & West Dartmoor
- Stevenstone & Torrington Farmers Hunt
- Tetcott & South Tetcott Hunts
- Western Hunt

CENTRES

- Barguse Riding Centre
- Coker Brown School of Riding
- Great Trethew Trekking
- Hunterswood Riding and Livery Stables
- La Rocco Riding School
- Lakefield Equestrian Centre
- Lauras Lessons
- Little Margate Equestrian
- Lower Tokenbury Equestrian Centre
- Newton Ferrers Equus
- St Leonards Equitation Centre

AREA 17

Area Representative: Fran Rowlatt-McCormick
area17@pcuk.org
07912 627751

Centre Coordinator: Colleen Glasgow
area17.centres@pcuk.org
07885 800813

BRANCHES

- East Antrim
- East Down
- Fermanagh Harriers
- Iveagh
- Killultagh Old Rock & Chichester Harriers
- Mid Antrim
- North Derry
- North Down
- Route Hunt
- Seskinore Harriers
- Tullylagan

CENTRES

- Birr House Riding Centre
- City of Derry Equestrian Centre
- Faughanvale Stables
- Laurel View Equestrian Centre
- Lodge Equine Stables
- RD Equestrian
- Smile Equestrian
- St Patricks Way Stables
- Tullymurray Equestrian Centre

AREA 18

Area Representative: Julie Hodson
area18@pcuk.org
01239 654314

Centre Coordinator: Emma Coates
area18.centres@pcuk.org
07973 677820

BRANCHES

- Amman Valley & District
- Banwen & District
- Carmarthen Bay
- Gogerddan
- Llandeilo & District
- Neath
- Parc Howard
- Pembrokeshire Hunt
- South Pembrokeshire & Cresselly Hunt
- Swansea & District
- Tivyside
- Vale of Clettwr
- Vale of Taf

CENTRES

- Bowlings Riding School
- Cefngranod Stables
- Cimla Trekking and Equestrian Centre
- Clyne Farm Centre
- Dinefwr Riding Centre
- Green Farm Riding Stables
- Havard Stables
- Rheidol Riding Centre

AREA 19

Area Representative: Anne Ekin
area19@pcuk.org
07711 630433

Centre Coordinator: Sarah Lewins
area19.centres@pcuk.org
07799 404246

BRANCHES

- Argyll South
- Berwickshire Hunt
- Dalkeith & District
- Duke of Buccleuch's Hunt
- Dumfriesshire Hunt
- East Lothian
- Edinburgh
- Eglinton Hunt
- Eskdale
- Galloway
- Isle of Mull
- Lanark & Upperward
- Lanarkshire & Renfrewshire Hunt
- Lauderdale Hunt
- Linlithgow & Stirlingshire
- Nithsdale
- Peebles Tweeddale
- Stewartry
- Strathblane & District

CENTRES

- Argyll Adventure
- Fergushill Riding Stables
- Fordbank Equestrian Centre
- Tannoch Stables
- Wardhouse Equestrian Centre
- Wellsfield Equestrian Centre

PONY CLUB BRANCHES IN THE UK

Founding Branches are denoted by a sideline next to their name

Aberconwy (1974)
Area 5
aberconwy@pcuk.org
DC Jessica Foulkes-Kelly
SEC Gwawr Williams

Albrighton Hunt (1933)
Area 7
albrighton@pcuk.org
DC Rory Howard
SEC Helen Howard

Albrighton Woodland Hunt (1932)
Area 7
albrightonwoodland@pcuk.org
DC Trevor Brighton
SEC Amy Conway

Amman Valley & District (1966)
Area 18
ammanvalley@pcuk.org
DC Elizabeth Ivey
SEC Louise Evans

Anglesey (1984)
Area 5
anglesey@pcuk.org
DC Jill Owen
SEC Louise Richardson

Angus (1949)
Area 1
angus@pcuk.org
DC Kirsty Geddes
SEC Tricia Hynd

Argyll South (1980)
Area 19
argyllsouth@pcuk.org
DC Gillian MacVicar
SEC Elizabeth Anne MacNab

Ashford Valley (1934)
Area 11
ashfordvalley@pcuk.org
DC Philippa Jones
SEC Sarah Castro-Edwards

Atherstone Hunt (1931)
Area 7
atherstone@pcuk.org
DC Emma Neal
SEC Charlotte Mawdesley

Avon Vale (1947)
Area 14
avonvale@pcuk.org
DC Helen Milne-Day
SEC Laura Emerson

Axe Vale Hunt (1958)
Area 15
axevale@pcuk.org
DC Danielle Jones
SEC Sarah Tulloch

Badsworth Hunt (1930)
Area 3
badsworth@pcuk.org
DC Charlie Warde-Aldam
SEC Wendy Truelove

Banwell (1960)
Area 14
banwell@pcuk.org
DC Imogen Rogers-Nash
SEC Verity Wring

Banwen & District (1956)
Area 18
banwen@pcuk.org
DC Chris Powell
SEC Dennis Whitney

Barlow Hunt (1934)
Area 6
barlow@pcuk.org
DC Liz Lovell
SEC Claire Lambie

Beaufort Hunt (1932)
Area 9
beaufort@pcuk.org
DC Alex Harbottle
DC Marianne Edwards
SEC Abigail Sharp

Bedale & West of Yore Hunt (1933)
Area 3
bedalewestofyores@pcuk.org
DC Alison Bartle
DC Karen Black
SEC Karen Black

Bedfordshire South (1935)
Area 12
bedfordshiresouth@pcuk.org
DC Sylvia Millard
SEC Chrissy Bury

Belvoir Hunt (1930)
Area 6
belvoir@pcuk.org
DC Tessa Buckley
SEC Samantha Campbell

Bennachie (1981)
Area 1
bennachie@pcuk.org
DC Liz Craigie
SEC Kirsten Douglas

Berkeley Hunt (1930)
Area 9
berkeley@pcuk.org
DC Holly Dowsing
SEC Paula Clarke

Berkeley South (1979)
Area 9
berkeleysouth@pcuk.org
DC Nikki Hiseman
DC Lisa Horder
SEC Judy Hicks

Berwickshire Hunt (1932)
Area 19
berwickshire@pcuk.org
DC Tamara Inness
SEC Gemma McDougall

Berwyn & Dee (1974)
Area 5
berwyndee@pcuk.org
DC Valerie Ann Edwards
SEC Holly Roe

Bicester & Warden Hill Hunt (1930)
Area 12
bicesterandwardenhill@pcuk.org
DC Julie Gordon
SEC Alexandra Machin

Bisley and Sandown Chase (2013)
Area 13
bisley@pcuk.org
DC Anne-Marie Bibby
DC Jemma Saunders-Byrne
SEC Anne-Marie Bibby

Blackburn & District (1965)
Area 4
blackburn@pcuk.org
DC Elaine Barker
SEC Helen Atkinson

Blackmore & Sparkford Vale Hunt (1930)
Area 14
blackmoreandsparkfordvale@pcuk.org
DC Veryan Gould

Blankney Hunt (1938)
Area 6
blankney@pcuk.org
DC Anthea Jepson
SEC Jessica Lovett

Braes of Derwent South (1982)
Area 2
braesofd@pcuk.org
DC Alex Emmerson
SEC Lindsay Sheridan

Bramham Moor Hunt (1932)
Area 3
bramhammoor@pcuk.org
DC Elizabeth Hughes
SEC Emma Harris

Brecon & Talybont Hunt (1950)
Area 10
breconandtalybont@pcuk.org
DC Ceri Bevan
DC Antonia Sheppard
SEC Amber Delahooke

Brocklesby Hunt (1944)
Area 6
brocklesby@pcuk.org
DC Amy Baylis
SEC Mandy Ross

Burghley (1958)
Area 6
burghley@pcuk.org
DC Laura Leicester
SEC Clare Blackwell

Burton Cheshire Forest (1948)
Area 5
burtoncheshireforest@pcuk.org
DC Cathy Church
SEC Nicky Fryer

Burton Hunt (1947)
Area 6
burton@pcuk.org
DC Charlotte Fursdon
DC Rosie Newsam
SEC Kerry Bailey

Caithness (1973)
Area 1
caithness@pcuk.org
DC Lisa Kennedy
SEC Elizabeth Hewitson

Cambridgeshire Hunt (1934)
Area 8
cambridgeshire@pcuk.org
DC Emily Casey
SEC Helen Zwetsloot

Carmarthen Bay (1983)
Area 18
carmarthenbay@pcuk.org
DC Tim Joynson
SEC Kirsten Davies

Cattistock Hunt (1931)
Area 14
cattistock@pcuk.org
DC Tessa Mackenzie-Green
SEC Susan Harris

Cheshire Hunt North (1930)
Area 5
cheshirenorth@pcuk.org
DC Natalie Cliffe
DC Sarah Le Grys
SEC Julie Pedley

Cheshire Hunt South (1950)
Area 5
cheshiresouth@pcuk.org
DC Chris Kirby
SEC Karen Kirk

Chiddingfold (1930)
Area 13
chiddingfold@pcuk.org
DC Liz Cross
SEC Lucy Jackson

Chiddingfold Farmers (1949)
Area 13
chiddingfoldfarmers@pcuk.org
DC Annette Hammond
SEC Annette Hammond

Chipping (1977)
Area 4
chipping@pcuk.org
DC Joanne Conlon
SEC Daphne Garment

Cleveland Hunt (1935)
Area 2
cleveland@pcuk.org
DC Vikki Clark
SEC Fiona Campbell

Cobham and Wimbledon (1951)
Area 11
wimbledon@pcuk.org
DC Cathy McGettigan
DC Elizabeth Jackson
SEC Michelle Agate

Cotley Hunt (1946)
Area 15
cotley@pcuk.org
DC Caroline Ford
SEC Liz Russo

Cotswold (1930)
Area 9
cotswold@pcuk.org
DC Lucy Garbutt
SEC Arabella Clarkson

Cotswold Vale Farmers' Hunt (1952)
Area 9
cotswoldvalefarmers@pcuk.org
DC Christina Dee
DC Jane Haslum
SEC Helen Dean

Cottesmore Hunt (1929)
Area 6
cottesmore@pcuk.org
DC Emily McLane
SEC Mary Tait

Cowdray Hunt (1936)
Area 13
cowdray@pcuk.org
DC Fiona Moss

Craven Hunt (1929)
Area 14
craven@pcuk.org
DC Vicky Welch
DC Kerry Cox
SEC Alison Wellman

Crawley & Horsham Hunt (1932)
Area 11
crawleyhorsham@pcuk.org
DC Julia Martin
SEC Angela Ellis

Crawley & Horsham Hunt South (1969)
Area 13
crawleyhorshamsouth@pcuk.org
DC Elisa Franks
Sec Lyn Baker

Crickhowell & District (1982)
Area 10
crickhowell@pcuk.org
DC Hannah Laurent
SEC Rebecca Faulkner

Croome Hunt (1931)
Area 9
croome@pcuk.org
DC Sarah Roberts
SEC Jane Ogle

Cumberland Farmers' Hunt (South) (1943)
Area 2
cumberlandfarmerssouth@pcuk.org
DC Sarah Harden
SEC Fiona Veitch

Cumberland Farmers Hunt North (1949)
Area 2
cumberlandfarmersnorth@pcuk.org
DC Alison Gribbon
SEC Fiona Wharton

Cumberland Foxhounds (1957)
Area 2
cumberlandfoxhounds@pcuk.org
DC Cerita Trafford

Curre Hunt (1958)
Area 10
curre@pcuk.org
DC Jackie Budd
SEC Vicky Cardale

Cury Hunt (1979)
Area 16
cury@pcuk.org
DC Karen Hurst
SEC Beth Haslam

Dalkeith & District (1963)
Area 19
dalkeith@pcuk.org
DC Tracy Dow
SEC Julie McLeish

Dare Valley (1999)
Area 10
darevalley@pcuk.org
DC Michelle Lewis
SEC Nicola Morgan

Dartmoor (1935)
Area 16
dartmoor@pcuk.org
DC Jane Mumford
SEC Amanda Kemsley

Deeside (1977)
Area 1
deeside@pcuk.org
DC Mary Robertson
SEC Nicola Macnab

Derwent Hunt (1963)
Area 3
derwent@pcuk.org
DC Lynne Harrison
SEC Elaine McNichol

Deveron (1973)
Area 1
deveron@pcuk.org
DC Karen Watson
SEC Anna Renouf

Devon & Somerset (1931)
Area 15
devonsomerset@pcuk.org
DC Karen Illing
SEC Sarah Daniel

Dinas Powys (1975)
Area 10
dinaspowis@pcuk.org
DC Clare Roberts
SEC Ceri Rowlands

Dolgellau & District (2009)
Area 5
dolgellau@pcuk.org
DC Sarah Meredith
SEC Ceri Jones

Duke of Buccleuch's Hunt (1931)
Area 19
dukeofbuccleuchs@pcuk.org
DC Karen Marshall
SEC Emma Catlin

Dulverton West Foxhounds (North Molton) Hunt (1957)
Area 15
dulvertonwestfoxhoundsnorthmolton@pcuk.org
DC Sara Gallagher
SEC Donna Wright

Dumfriesshire Hunt (1932)
Area 19
dumfriesshire@pcuk.org
DC Nicola Kerr

Dwyfor and Gwynedd (2022)
Area 5
dwyfor@pcuk.org
DC Francess Ifan

East Aberdeenshire (Buchan) (1977)
Area 1
eastaberdeenshirebuchan@pcuk.org
DC Donna Wiseman
SEC Donna Wiseman

East Antrim (1965)
Area 17
eastantrim@pcuk.org
DC Hayley Cunningham
SEC Kathy Morrow

East Cheshire (1960)
Area 5
eastcheshire@pcuk.org
DC Geoff Bell
SEC Eloise Miller

East Cornwall Hunt (1931)
Area 16
eastcornwall@pcuk.org
DC Helen Moore (16)
SEC Deborah Glover

East Devon Hunt (1932)
Area 15
eastdevon@pcuk.org
DC Martine Conneeley
DC Clare Leonard
SEC Kirsty O'Dell

East Down (1936)
Area 17
eastdown@pcuk.org
DC Margaret Newsam
SEC Christine Crozier

East Essex (1932)
Area 8
eastessex@pcuk.org
DC Kate Tabor
SEC Clair Dawson

East Hertfordshire Hunt (1931)
Area 12
easthertfordshire@pcuk.org
DC Trish Griffiths
SEC Lisa Garrad

East Kent Hunt (1933)
Area 11
eastkent@pcuk.org
DC Anita Head
SEC Katie Latchford

East Lothian (1952)
Area 19
eastlothian@pcuk.org
DC Lorna Harvey
SEC Laura Cull Hooker

East Stirlingshire (1970)
Area 1
eaststirlingshire@pcuk.org
DC Judi Dunn
DC Kaeli Pettigrew
SEC Kaeli Pettigrew

East Sussex (1931)
Area 11
eastsussex@pcuk.org
DC Louise Coppard
SEC Debbie Lapworth

Easton Harriers Hunt (1935)
Area 8
easton@pcuk.org
DC Helena Packshaw
SEC Caroline Foster

Edinburgh (1994)
Area 19
edinburgh@pcuk.org
DC Katie Pier
SEC Kellyanne Miller

Eggesford Hunt (1951)
Area 16
eggesford@pcuk.org
DC Deborah Handley
SEC Shouna Sibcy

Eglinton Hunt (1933)
Area 19
eglinton@pcuk.org
DC Pamela Johnstone
SEC Alison King

Enfield Chace Hunt (1933)
Area 8
enfieldchace@pcuk.org
DC Vicky Justice
SEC Sally Hawes

Eridge (1935)
Area 11
eridge@pcuk.org
DC Sophie Chambers
SEC Sarah Davies

Eskdale (1974)
Area 19
eskdale@pcuk.org
DC Hannah Robertson
SEC christine ewart

Essex & Suffolk Hunt (1939)
Area 8
essexsuffolk@pcuk.org
DC Mary Thornley
SEC Sophie Bardrick

Essex Farmers (1960)
Area 8
essexfarmers@pcuk.org
DC Philippa Howie
DC Emma Rushen
SEC Kirsten Mackay

Essex Hunt North (1956)
Area 8
essexnorth@pcuk.org
DC Joanne Haigh
SEC Rebecca Willis

Essex Union (1930)
Area 8
essexunion@pcuk.org
DC Emma Whiteford
SEC Shireen Clark

Essex Union South (1968)
Area 8
essexunionsouth@pcuk.org
DC Lucy Brockway-Smith

Fermanagh Harriers (1956)
Area 17
fermanagh@pcuk.org
DC Frances Rolston Bruce
SEC Denise Owens

Fernie Hunt (1929)
Area 6
fernie@pcuk.org
DC
SEC Claire Robinson

Fife Hunt (1946)
Area 1
fife@pcuk.org
DC Jane MacLeod
SEC Fiona Morrison

Fitzwilliam Hunt (1930)
Area 6
fitzwilliam@pcuk.org
DC Philippa Patel
SEC Sylvie Hall

Flamstead (1973)
Area 12
flamstead@pcuk.org
DC Rosie Grimston
SEC Gemma Issott

Flint & Denbigh Hunt (1947)
Area 5
flintdenbigh@pcuk.org
DC Bethan Jones
SEC Iona Pierce

Forth Valley (1960)
Area 1
forthvalley@pcuk.org
DC Ainsley Leitch
SEC Tracey Cooper

Four Burrow Hunt (1935)
Area 16
fourburrow@pcuk.org
DC Peter Murrish
SEC Gill Whetman

Furness & District (1949)
Area 4
furness@pcuk.org
DC Cathy Almond
SEC Lindsey Wiejak

Fylde & District (1957)
Area 4
fylde@pcuk.org
DC Elizabeth Jackson

Galloway (1957)
Area 19
galloway@pcuk.org
DC Joss Drummond
SEC Susie Petrucci

Garth Hunt (1930)
Area 13
garth@pcuk.org
DC lucy cochrane
SEC Janet Yelloly

Garth South (1965)
Area 13
garthsouth@pcuk.org
DC Candy Burnyeat
SEC Candy Burnyeat

Glaisdale Hunt (1966)
Area 3
glaisdale@pcuk.org
DC Jenny Fowles
SEC Gill Kidd

Glamorgan Hunt (1949)
Area 10
glamorgan@pcuk.org
DC Annie Whitehouse
SEC Sian Dix

Glenrothes (1978)
Area 1
glenrothes@pcuk.org
DC Alison Peden
SEC Lucy Orr

Glossop & District (1972)
Area 4
glossop@pcuk.org
DC Alison Mackinnon
SEC Emma McCallum

Gogerddan (1956)
Area 18
gogerddan@pcuk.org
DC Heather Pagan
SEC Sarah Jones

Golden Valley (1946)
Area 10
goldenvalley@pcuk.org
DC Netty Greenow
DC Kate Ebery
SEC Billie Jones

Goodwood (1989)
Area 13
goodwood@pcuk.org
DC Charlotte Butterworth
SEC Elizabeth McGregor

Grafton Hunt (1930)
Area 12
grafton@pcuk.org
DC Carolyn Harvey
SEC Laura Hawkins

Grove Hunt (1945)
Area 6
grove@pcuk.org
DC Emma Marsden
SEC Kennedy Taylor-Camm

Guernsey (1954)
Area 14
guernsey@pcuk.org
SEC Brenda De Carteret

Hambledon Hunt (North) (1946)
Area 13
hambledonnorth@pcuk.org
DC Sarah Mosse
DC Victoria Cobden
SEC Marianne Fisher

Hampshire Hunt (1931)
Area 13
hh@pcuk.org
DC Nicola Rowsell
SEC Cathryn Hewett

Haydock Park (1958)
Area 4
haydockpark@pcuk.org
DC Michelle Beard
SEC Shirley Green

Heart of England (1975)
Area 7
heartofengland@pcuk.org
DC Shelley Mitchell
SEC Sue Hall

Hertfordshire Hunt (1934)
Area 12
hertfordshire@pcuk.org
DC Amelia Clow
SEC Zoe Vaughan

Heythrop Hunt (1931)
Area 9
heythrop@pcuk.org
DC Kate Campion
DC Nicola Browne
SEC Lori Vokes

High Peak Hunt (1932)
Area 6
highpeak@pcuk.org
DC Ruth Taylor
SEC Ann Kenworthy

Holcombe Hunt (1931)
Area 4
holcombe@pcuk.org
DC Lesley Jenkinson
SEC Charlotte Staines

Holderness Hunt (1946)
Area 3
holderness@pcuk.org
DC Pamela Ireland
SEC Deborah Bayliss

Hursley Hunt (1946)
Area 14
hursley@pcuk.org
DC Stuart Robertson
SEC Sheila Robertson

Hurworth Hunt (1933)
Area 3
hurworth@pcuk.org
DC Louisa Hunter
SEC Louisa Hunter

Inverness-shire (1964)
Area 1
inverness-shire@pcuk.org
DC Carlann Mackay
DC Amanda Campbell
SEC Jenna Hesling

Irfon & Tywi (2001)
Area 10
irfontywi@pcuk.org
DC Jo Price
SEC Jo Price

Isle of Man (1958)
Area 4
isleofman@pcuk.org
DC Alice Corrin
DC Cheryl Curphey
SEC Zoe Huxham

Isle of Mull (1976)
Area 19
isleofmull@pcuk.org
DC Flora Corbett
SEC Camrie Maclennan

Isle of Wight (1931)
Area 13
isleofwight@pcuk.org
DC Kirsty Snodgrass
SEC Kate Cockle

Iveagh (1962)
Area 17
iveagh@pcuk.org
DC John Kehoe
SEC Cathy Robinson

Ivel Valley (1981)
Area 12
ivelvalley@pcuk.org
DC Caroline Warwick
DC Jessica Kelly
SEC Jenny Knight

Jersey Drag Hunt (1952)
Area 14
jerseydrag@pcuk.org
DC Pippa Webster
SEC Sophie Oliveira

Kenfig Hill (2017)
Area 10
kenfighill@pcuk.org
DC Alison Davies
SEC Laura Terry

Kent Border (1980)
Area 11
kentborder@pcuk.org
DC Jo True
SEC Katherine Ingleby

Killultagh Old Rock & Chichester Harriers (1959)
Area 17
killultagh@pcuk.org
DC Noreen Fitzpatrick
SEC Jenny Rollins

Kincardineshire (1963)
Area 1
kincardineshire@pcuk.org
DC Janice Carnegie
SEC Victoria Dolin

Lamerton Hunt (1954)
Area 16
lamerton@pcuk.org
DC Sue Ryan
SEC Sally Jennings

Lanark & Upperward (1974)
Area 19
lanarkupperward@pcuk.org
DC Margaret Young
SEC Kirstie MacGillivray

Lanarkshire & Renfrewshire Hunt (1934)
Area 19
lanarkshirerenfrewshire@pcuk.org
DC Tom Alexander

Lancaster & District (1964)
Area 4
lancaster@pcuk.org
DC Emma Walsh

Lauderdale Hunt (1982)
Area 19
lauderdale@pcuk.org
DC Gillian Mcfadyen
SEC Gillian Mcfadyen

Ledbury Hunt (1932)
Area 9
ledbury@pcuk.org
DC Sophie Jones
SEC Katie Baker

Linlithgow & Stirlingshire (1931)
Area 19
linlithgowstirlingshire@pcuk.org
DC Clare McLay
DC Claire Leitch
SEC Caroline Courtney

Littleport & District (1970)
Area 8
littleport@pcuk.org
DC Darryl Preston
SEC Anne Hall

Llandeilo & District (1982)
Area 18
llandeilo@pcuk.org
DC Karen Goss
DC Patricia Hearn
SEC Karen Goss

Llangeinor Hunt (1960)
Area 10
llangeinor@pcuk.org
DC Rachel Pugh
DC Lesley Kemeys
SEC Louise Owen

Lord Leconfield Hunt (1934)
Area 13
lordleconfield@pcuk.org
DC Clare Emery
DC Sue Coombe Tennant
SEC Carrie Schroter

Ludlow Hunt (1929)
Area 7
ludlow@pcuk.org
DC Louise Powell
SEC Jean Yarnold

Malvern (1940)
Area 9
malvern@pcuk.org
DC Maria Hardy
SEC Amanda Allsop

Mendip Farmers' Hunt (1930)
Area 14
mendipfarmers@pcuk.org
DC Wendy Smith
SEC Diana Tincknell

Meynell (1929)
Area 6
meynell@pcuk.org
DC Lesley Cutler
SEC Elizabeth Ovenden

Mid Antrim (1971)
Area 17
midantrim@pcuk.org
DC Rachelle Mark
SEC Elizabeth Rankin

Mid Devon Hunt (1937)
Area 16
middevon@pcuk.org
DC Frances Haywood Smith
SEC Frances Haywood Smith

Mid Surrey (1931)
Area 11
midsurrey@pcuk.org
DC Gina Kitchener
DC Naomi Kitchener
SEC Wendy Wrist

Middleton Hunt (1932)
Area 3
middleton@pcuk.org
DC Trish Russell
SEC Sarah Jane Barker

Middleton Hunt (East Side) (1975)
Area 3
middletoneastside@pcuk.org
DC Helen Milner
SEC Kim Rothwell

Minchinhampton (1969)
Area 9
minchinhampton@pcuk.org
DC Julie Crew
SEC Thandi Rudin

Monmouthshire (1931)
Area 10
monmouthshire@pcuk.org
DC Susan Fairweather
SEC Jessica Tod

Moray & Nairn (1948)
Area 1
moraynairn@pcuk.org
DC Hayley Ingram
SEC Mary Lindsay

Morpeth Hunt (1937)
Area 2
morpeth@pcuk.org
DC Michelle Macaulay
SEC Gail Jeffrey

Neath (1968)
Area 18
neath@pcuk.org
DC Ceinwen Howells
SEC Angela Tucker

New Forest Hunts (1932)
Area 14
newforest@pcuk.org
DC Susan Mitchell
SEC Susan Hogarth

Newcastle & North Durham (1961)
Area 2
newcastlenorthdurham@pcuk.org
DC Sheila Clifford
SEC Melanie Boatman

Newmarket & Thurlow Hunt (1940)
Area 8
newmarketthurlow@pcuk.org
DC Tessa Vestey
SEC Belinda Hull

Nithsdale (1978)
Area 19
nithsdale@pcuk.org
DC Philippa Barnes
SEC Dawn Murdoch

North Argyll (1968)
Area 1
northargyll@pcuk.org
DC Janice Burnip
SEC Laura MacGregor

North Cornwall (1932)
Area 16
northcornwall@pcuk.org
DC Anita Foulsham

North Cotswold Hunt (1930)
Area 9
northcotswold@pcuk.org
DC Jackie Ferguson
SEC Paula Leavy

North Derry (1950)
Area 17
northderry@pcuk.org
DC Pauline Lusby
SEC Laura ONeill

North Down (1939)
Area 17
northdown@pcuk.org
DC Evelyn Dunlop
SEC Cheryl Wallace

North Herefordshire Hunt (1951)
Area 9
northherefordshire@pcuk.org
DC Charlotte Thomas
SEC Vici Morse

North Norfolk (1935)
Area 8
northnorfolk@pcuk.org
DC Emma Papworth
SEC Holly Alston

North Northumberland Hunt (1955)
Area 2
northnorthumberland@pcuk.org
DC Catherine Armstrong
DC Melanie Lowdon-King
SEC Jane Mason

North Shropshire Hunt (1929)
Area 7
northshropshire@pcuk.org
DC Ann Gregory
SEC Ann Gregory

North Staffordshire Hunt (1931)
Area 7
northstaffordshire@pcuk.org
DC Natalie Massey
SEC Rebecca Mayer

North Warwickshire (1931)
Area 7
northwarwickshire@pcuk.org
DC Elizabeth Grindal
SEC Linda Wolverson

Oakley Hunt North (1981)
Area 12
oakleynorth@pcuk.org
DC Christine Cinnamond
SEC Clare Goduti

Oakley Hunt West (1931)
Area 12
oakleywest@pcuk.org
DC Wendy Barnes
SEC Fiona Falle

Old Berkeley Hunt (Chilterns) (1968)
Area 12
oldberkeleychilterns@pcuk.org
DC Emma Stratford
SEC Katie Bowden

Old Berkeley Hunt (Hughenden) (1968)
Area 12
oldberkeleyhughenden@pcuk.org
DC Amanda Bacon
SEC Juliette Knott

Old Berkeley Hunt (North) (1959)
Area 12
oldberkeleynorth@pcuk.org
DC Sue Palmer-Shaw
DC Catherine Cawdron
SEC Sarah Molony

Old Berkeley Hunt (South) (1959)
Area 12
oldberkeleysouth@pcuk.org
DC Kim Williams
SEC Jessica Latimer

Old Berkshire Hunt (1943)
Area 9
oldberkshire@pcuk.org
DC Lisa Powell
SEC Helen Keen

Old Surrey & Burstow Hunt (1929)
Area 11
oldsurreyburstow@pcuk.org
DC Caroline Matthews
DC Melissa Beatty
SEC Amanda Bernard

Orkney (1963)
Area 1
orkney@pcuk.org
DC Carole Linklater
SEC Karen Johnston

Oxenholme (1936)
Area 4
oxenholme@pcuk.org
DC Jillian Clark
SEC Karen Barnes

Parc Howard (1993)
Area 18
parchoward@pcuk.org
DC Catherine Roberts
SEC Marie Launchbury

Peak (1959)
Area 4
peak@pcuk.org
DC Danielle Dawson
SEC Lynne Wilmot

Peebles Tweeddale (1975)
Area 19
peeblestweeddale@pcuk.org
DC Kate Philipps
SEC Nicola Spurway

Pembrokeshire Hunt (1935)
Area 18
pembrokeshire@pcuk.org
DC Janet Luke
DC Jill Ridge
SEC Sally Evans

Pendle Forest & Craven Hunt (1935)
Area 4
pendleforestcraven@pcuk.org
DC Elizabeth Bower

Pentyrch (1953)
Area 10
pentyrch@pcuk.org
DC Lynda Evans
SEC Sue DuCroq

Percy Hunt (1947)
Area 2
percy@pcuk.org
DC Sue Haughie
SEC Susie McDonald

Perth Hunt (1946)
Area 1
perth@pcuk.org
DC Genna Dall
SEC Alison Craig

Petersfield (1977)
Area 13
petersfield@pcuk.org
DC Gill Ibbott
SEC Julie Gordon

Polden Hills (1975)
Area 15
poldenhills@pcuk.org
DC Kim Tripp
SEC Lorraine Wells

Poole & District (1973)
Area 14
poole@pcuk.org
DC Sarah Chandler
DC Cheryl Dennett
SEC Lynne Seare

Portman Hunt (1931)
Area 14
portman@pcuk.org
DC Linda Jones
SEC Vanessa Sherry

Puckeridge Hunt (1931)
Area 8
puckeridge@pcuk.org
DC Sophie Payne
SEC Jennifer Snell

Puckeridge Hunt Western (1946)
Area 8
puckeridgewestern@pcuk.org
DC Emma Hogg
DC Sue Underhill

Pytchley Hunt (1930)
Area 7
pytchley@pcuk.org
DC Sarah Jane Page
SEC Elise Paybody

Quantock Hunt (1933)
Area 15
quantock@pcuk.org
DC Kathryn Sims
SEC Kaye Hill

Quorn Hunt (1929)
Area 6
quorn@pcuk.org
DC Julie Mann
SEC Carol Davis

Radnor & West Hereford Hunt (1935)
Area 10
radnor@pcuk.org

Rockwood Harriers (1930)
Area 3
rockwood@pcuk.org

Romney Marsh (1948)
Area 11
romneymarsh@pcuk.org
DC Christine Makin
SEC Sarah Hues

Ross-shire (1959)
Area 1
ross-shire@pcuk.org
DC Yvonne Maclean
SEC Karen Cameron

Route Hunt (1958)
Area 17
route@pcuk.org
DC Karen Woodrow
DC Fred White
SEC Patricia van Veen

Royal Artillery (1946)
Area 14
ra@pcuk.org
DC Judy Hyson

Rufford Hunt (1948)
Area 6
rufford@pcuk.org
DC Debbie Dawson
SEC Diane Shepheard

Ryburn Valley (1970)
Area 3
ryburnvalley@pcuk.org
DC Liz Dunn
SEC Louise Jones

Saddleworth & District (1960)
Area 4
saddleworth@pcuk.org
DC Gill Morrell
SEC Stephanie McMillan

Scunthorpe & District (1968)
Area 6
scunthorpe@pcuk.org
DC Lisa Auchterlonie
SEC James Rowland

Seavington (1974)
Area 15
seavington@pcuk.org
DC Pip Bailey
DC Paul Bailey
SEC Hayley Pattemore

Sennybridge & District (1974)
Area 10
sennybridge@pcuk.org
DC Georgina Philipson-Stow
SEC Susan Moore

Seskinore Harriers (1974)
Area 17
seskinore@pcuk.org
DC Mandy McQuade
DC Jenna Coote
SEC Bernie Murnaghan

Silverton Hunt (1931)
Area 15
silverton@pcuk.org
DC Claire Cook

Sinnington Hunt (1946)
Area 3
sinnington@pcuk.org
DC Ruth Smith
SEC Ailsa Teasdale

The Wynnstay (1929)
Area 5
sirwwwynns@pcuk.org
DC Belinda Hutchinson Smith
DC Joanna Adams
SEC Jane Courtney

Soham & District (1976)
Area 8
soham@pcuk.org
DC Sally Green
SEC Charlotte Gunbie

South & West Wilts Hunt (1934)
Area 14
southwestwilts@pcuk.org
DC Henrietta Woodward
SEC Sarah Wilkinson

South Berkshire (1930)
Area 13
southberkshire@pcuk.org
DC Camilla Gilchrist
SEC Emily Mumby

South Devon Hunt (Moorland) (1973)
Area 16
southdevonmoorland@pcuk.org
DC Fiona Froy
SEC Della Irish

South Devon West (1932)
Area 16
southdevonwest@pcuk.org
DC Heather Venmore

South Dorset Hunt (1931)
Area 14
southdorset@pcuk.org
DC Leonie Murfin
SEC Alice Haw

South Durham Hunt (1947)
Area 2
southdurham@pcuk.org
DC Brenda Gray
SEC Emma-Kate Darnton

South Hereford and Ross Harriers (1944)
Area 9
southherefordross@pcuk.org
DC Kirstie Macfarlane
SEC Julia Hay

South Hertfordshire (1963)
Area 12
southhertfordshire@pcuk.org
DC Samantha Branley
SEC Melanie Reid

South Norfolk (1935)
Area 8
southnorfolk@pcuk.org
DC Aidan Taylor
SEC Sue Taylor

South Northumberland (1931)
Area 2
southnorthumberland@pcuk.org
DC Mary Ann Reay
SEC Sara Stewart

South Nottinghamshire (1939)
Area 6
southnottinghamshire@pcuk.org
DC Jane Clayton
SEC Janet Rycroft

South Oxfordshire Hunt (South) (1930)
Area 12
southoxfordshiresouth@pcuk.org
DC Louise Pope
SEC Bonnie Larcombe

South Oxfordshire Hunt Central (1961)
Area 12
southoxfordshirecentral@pcuk.org
DC Tamsin Woods
SEC Rachel Miller

South Pembrokeshire & Cresselly Hunt (1958)
Area 18
southpembrokeshire@pcuk.org
DC Catherine Nicholas
SEC Caroline Elsdon

South Pool (1963)
Area 16
southpool@pcuk.org
DC Margaret Brooks
SEC Ellen Seccombe

South Shropshire Hunt (1929)
Area 7
southshropshire@pcuk.org
DC Tor Smith
SEC Verity Criddle

South Staffordshire Hunt (1931)
Area 7
southstaffordshire@pcuk.org
DC Katharine Egerton
SEC Jennie Barker

South Trent (1963)
Area 6
southtrent@pcuk.org
DC Jane Foster
SEC Genevieve Stewart-Smith

South Wold Hunt North (1950)
Area 6
southwoldnorth@pcuk.org
DC Krystina Alex
DC Lindy Robertson
SEC Karen Elliott

Southdown Hunt (East) (1976)
Area 11
southdowneast@pcuk.org
DC (Caroline) Anne Cook
SEC Candy Robbins

Southdown West (1936)
Area 11
southdownwest@pcuk.org
DC Tracy Vardy
DC Penny Harlington
SEC Anita Bucknall

Spooners & West Dartmoor (1967)
Area 16
spooners@pcuk.org
DC Rebecca Townsend
SEC Nicky Alford

St Davids & District (1984)
Area 18
saintdavids@pcuk.org
DC Rob Harper
SEC Judith Harper

Staff College & Sandhurst (1953)
Area 13
staffcollege@pcuk.org
DC Jane Austen Armstrong
SEC Natasha Marshall

Staintondale Hunt (1958)
Area 3
staintondale@pcuk.org
DC Zoe Jenkins
SEC Beth Rickinson

Stevenstone & Torrington Farmers Hunt (1945)
Area 16
stevenstone@pcuk.org
DC Sarah Ellis
SEC Zoe Roach

Stewartry (1965)
Area 19
stewartry@pcuk.org
DC Sarah Burton
SEC Julia Graham

Strathblane & District (1949)
Area 19
strathblane@pcuk.org
DC Jocelyn Glennie
SEC Emily Hotchkiss

Strathearn (1949)
Area 1
strathearn@pcuk.org
DC Jane Cepok
SEC Claire Ellis

Stroud (1978)
Area 9
stroud@pcuk.org
DC Catie Howard
SEC Linny Gray

Suffolk Hunt (1932)
Area 8
suffolk@pcuk.org
DC Jane Crawford
SEC Leanne Livall

Surrey Union (1935)
Area 11
surreyunion@pcuk.org
DC Deborah Winchester
SEC Tania FORSDICK

Swansea & District (1949)
Area 18
swansea@pcuk.org
DC Ann Walter
SEC Jessica Higgs

Syston (1964)
Area 14
syston@pcuk.org
DC Marie Kelly
SEC Gina Dagger

Tanatside Hunt (1935)
Area 5
tanatside@pcuk.org
DC Elspeth Carr
SEC Ruth Jones

Taunton Vale (1932)
Area 15
tauntonvale@pcuk.org
DC Elizabeth Crew
SEC Rachel Holden

Taunton Vale Harriers (1972)
Area 15
tauntonvaleharriers@pcuk.org
DC Jacquie Rowcliffe
SEC Vicky Stilton

Tedworth Hunt (1930)
Area 14
tedworth@pcuk.org
DC Joss Dalrymple
DC Sophie Dalrymple
SEC Lorraine Perry

Teme Valley Hunt (1962)
Area 10
temevalley@pcuk.org
DC Sadie Rowan
SEC Mandy Baldwin

Tetcott & South Tetcott Hunts (1953)
Area 16
tetcottsouthtetcotts@pcuk.org
DC Georgina Brown
SEC Gabrielle McHenry

Thetford Chase (1961)
Area 8
thetfordchase@pcuk.org
DC Laura Clear
SEC Zoe Southgate

Tickham (1937)
Area 11
tickham@pcuk.org
DC Caroline De Lucy
DC Jane Henry
SEC Joanna Stone

Tiverton Hunt (1946)
Area 15
tiverton@pcuk.org
DC Natalie Wedden
SEC Julie Heal

Tivyside (1960)
Area 18
tivyside@pcuk.org
DC Karen Dobson
SEC Mariette Sibley

Tredegar Farmers Hunt (1948)
Area 10
tredegarfarmers@pcuk.org
DC Martha Byford-Brooks
DC Fiona Lewis

Tullylagan (1976)
Area 17
tullylagan@pcuk.org
DC Christine Kennedy
DC Colleen Glasgow
SEC Jillian O'Neill

Tynedale Hunt (1971)
Area 2
tynedale@pcuk.org
DC Wendy Murray
SEC Lesley Walby

United Pack (1932)
Area 7
unitedpack@pcuk.org
DC Rebecca Huffer
SEC Hilary Laing (Griggs)

Vale of Aylesbury Hunt (1931)
Area 12
valeofaylesbury@pcuk.org
DC Clive Mentiply-Johnson
SEC Kate Rolfe

Vale of Clettwr (1975)
Area 18
valeofclettwr@pcuk.org
DC Claire Morice
SEC Ruth Owen Lewis

Vale of Taf (1978)
Area 18
valeoftaf@pcuk.org
DC Penni Jones
SEC Penni Jones

Vale of York (1976)
Area 3
valeofyork@pcuk.org
DC Christine Dalby
SEC Barbara Lister

Vine (1934)
Area 13
vine@pcuk.org
DC Sarah Dance
SEC Emma Jonas

VWH Hunt (1930)
Area 9
vwh@pcuk.org
DC Georgie Davies
SEC Jo Ramage

Waen-y-Llyn (1974)
Area 5
waen-y-llyn@pcuk.org
DC Dani Tanton
SEC Helen Lakin

Walpole & District (2006)
Area 8
walpole@pcuk.org
SEC Lorna Hayes

Warwickshire Hunt (1932)
Area 7
warwickshire@pcuk.org
DC Susan Dancer
SEC Pauline Collings

Waveney Harriers (1934)
Area 8
waveney@pcuk.org
DC Stephen Barrett
SEC Sarah Canham

West Hants (1967)
Area 14
westhants@pcuk.org
DC Jo Morris
SEC Kate Louise Morris

West Kent (Sevenoaks) (1930)
Area 11
westkentsevenoaks@pcuk.org
DC Emma Sollis
SEC Helen Giddings

West Kent Meopham (1972)
Area 11
westkentmeopham@pcuk.org
DC Julie Dinnis
DC Suzanne Cleary
SEC Lizzie Carter-Griffiths

West Lancashire County (1933)
Area 4
westlancashirecounty@pcuk.org
DC Fiona Lace
SEC Elaine Wall

West Lancashire Ince Blundell (1933)
Area 4
westlancashireinceblundell@pcuk.org
DC Michelle Dudley
SEC Fiona Clague

West Midlands (1975)
Area 7
westmidlands@pcuk.org
DC Dee Bagnall
SEC Julie Hayward

West Norfolk (1935)
Area 8
westnorfolk@pcuk.org
DC Kate Cook
SEC Sophie Edwards

West Perthshire (1974)
Area 1
westperthshire@pcuk.org
DC David Lindsay
SEC Kim Stewart

West Somerset (1956)
Area 15
westsomerset@pcuk.org
DC Karin Harwood
SEC Kali Martin

West Warwickshire (1961)
Area 7
westwarwickshire@pcuk.org
DC Caroline Chadwick
SEC Lucy Jackson

Western Hunt (1935)
Area 16
western@pcuk.org
DC Diana Hardy
SEC Sarah Tieken

Western Isles (1981)
Area 1
westernIsles@pcuk.org
DC Mairi Fellows
SEC Leeann Hope

Weston Harriers Hunt (1932)
Area 15
weston@pcuk.org
DC Karen Pinn
SEC Helen Lovell

Whaddon Chase (1931)
Area 12
whaddonchase@pcuk.org
DC Nicola Thorne
SEC Ria Bond

Wheatland Hunt (1946)
Area 7
wheatland@pcuk.org
DC Hannah Williams
SEC Amanda Liddle

Wheelton & District (1974)
Area 4
wheelton@pcuk.org
DC Ian Nolan-Plunkett

Wilton Hunt (1933)
Area 14
wilton@pcuk.org
DC Sally Lefroy
SEC Fran Lockyer

Wokingham (1974)
Area 13
wokingham@pcuk.org
DC Julie Browne
SEC Suzy Turner

Woodland Hunt (1950)
Area 12
woodland@pcuk.org
DC Emma Dag

Woodland Pytchley Hunt (1931)
Area 6
woodlandpytchley@pcuk.org
DC Lucie Burges-Lumdsen
SEC Amber Coleman

Worcestershire Hunt (1931)
Area 9
worcestershire@pcuk.org
DC Eve Wood
SEC Rebecca Briggs

Wormwood Scrubs (1992)
Area 12
wormwoodscrubs@pcuk.org

Wylye Valley (1952)
Area 14
wylyevalley@pcuk.org
DC Miles Toulson-Clarke
Sec Amy Maidstone

Wyndham (1964)
Area 2
wyndham@pcuk.org
DC Maureen White
SEC Carole Smith

Wyre Forest (1975)
Area 9
wyreforest@pcuk.org
DC Alison Vincent
SEC Catherine MacDonald

Ynysybwl (1976)
Area 10
ynysybwl@pcuk.org
DC Beverley Haddock
SEC Emma Davies

York & Ainsty North (1950)
Area 3
yorkainstynorth@pcuk.org
DC Barbara Birchall
SEC Helen Vesty

York & Ainsty South (1959)
Area 3
yorkainstysouth@pcuk.org
DC Gill Chivers
SEC Suzanna Barker

Zetland Hunt (1932)
Area 2
zetland@pcuk.org
DC Andrea Bartlett
SEC Rebecca Farnaby

PONY CLUB CENTRES IN THE UK

Accrington Riding Centre (Area 4)
Lesley Walton, Rothwell Mill Farm, Miller Fold, Accrington, Lancashire, BB5 0NY.
01254 393563
lesleypaddy@hotmail.com

Aldborough Hall Equestrian Centre (Area 8)
Dawn Deamer, Alborough Road, North Ilford, Esses, IG2 7TE.
02085 901433
dawn.deamer@yahoo.co.uk

Almond Equestrian (Area 6)
Jayne Almond, Waterloo Lodge Farm, Baggrave Hall Road, Leicester, Leicestershire, LE7 9JB.
07808 555262
jayney.88@hotmail.com

Alstone Court Riding Establishment (Area 14)
Olivia March, Alstone Lane, Highbridge, Somerset, TA9 3DS.
07702 392120
alstonecourt@live.co.uk

Ampfield Riding School (Area 14)
Lower Farm, Lower Farm Lane, Ampfield, SO51 9DP,
01794 367570
enquiries@ampfieldridingstables.co.uk

Angel Riding Centre (Area 3)
Debbie Murphy, Morton Lane, Hambleton, Selby, North Yorkshire, YO8 9LE.
07833 500333
Angellivery@live.co.uk

Anglesey Riding Centre (Area 5)
Fay Josephy, Tal-y-Foel, Dwyran, Llanfairpwll, Anglesey, LL61 6LQ.
01248 430377
angleseyriding@gmail.com

Annabelles Equestrian (Area 8)
Annabelle Block, Hall Farm, Church Road, Henstead, Beccles, Suffolk, NR34 7LD.
01502 742303
annabelle_block@hotmail.com

Apollo Stables (Area 8)
Emma Spencer, Undley Road, Lakenheath, Suffolk, IP27 9BX.
07881415346
apollostables1@gmail.com

Appletree Stud (Area 7)
Julie Scott, Claydon, Banbury, Oxfordshire, OX17 1ET.
07517 068354
appletreestud@btinternet.com

Argyll Adventure (Area 19)
Annika Cameron, Argyll Adventure, Dalchenna Farm, Inveraray, Argyll, PA32 8XT.
01499 302611
info@argylladventure.com

Ashe Green Riding (Area 8)
Lisa Kelly, Shrubbery Farm, Ipswich Road, Woodbridge, Suffolk, IP13 7PS.
07730 747715
kelly.lisa@hotmail.co.uk

Asti Equestrian (Area 9)
Claire Lisi, Millaway Farm, Goosey, Faringdon, Oxfordshire, SN7 8PA.
01367 710288
astiequestrian@hotmail.com

Badshot Lea Equestrian Centre (Area 13)
Emily Lemon, Badshot Lea Equestrian Centre, Badshot Farm Lane, Farnham, Surrey, GU9 9HY.
01252 312838
badshotleaec@gmail.com

Ballawhetstone (Area 4)
Stella Hampton, Ballawhetstone Farm, Douglas Road, Ballabeg, IM9 4ED.
01624 825778
Stella.hampton@me.com

Barguse Riding Centre (Area 16)
Lisa Todd, The Grange, Lockengate, St Austell, Cornwall, PL26 8RU.
01208 831817
info@barguse.co.uk

Barnfield Riding School (Area 13)
Patsy Ann Rose, Parkfields Road, Kingston upon Thames, Surrey, KT2 5LL.
0208 546 3616
info@barnfieldridingschool.org

Barnfields Chingford Riding School (Area 8)
Sewardstone Road, Chingford, London, E4 7RH.
02085 295200
Barnfieldsridingstables@gmail.com

Barton Field Farm Equestrian Centre (Area 11)
Natalie Brown, Wingham Road, Littlebourne, Canterbury, Kent, CT3 1UP.
07770 331557
info@bffec.co.uk

Batley Hall Farm Riding Centre (Area 3)
Debbie Gaskin, Old Hall Road, Upper Batley, West Yorkshire, WF17 0AX.
07990502007
equusridingclub@ymail.com

Baylands Equestrian Centre (Area 12)
Rebecca Whittingham, Stockwood Park, Luton, Bedfordshire, LU1 4BH.
01582 720766
baylands.luton@gmail.com

Beaumont Grange Farm (Area 4)
Danielle Pritchard, Black Castle Lane, Off Bottom Dale Road, Slyne with Hest, Nr Lancaster, Lancashire, LA2 6BG.
07904 208669
carolhillbeaumontgrange@gmail.com

Beaver Hall (Area 7)
Ann Chadwick, Bradnop, Leek, Staffordshire, ST13 7EZ.
01538 304433
horses@beaverhall.co.uk

Berkshire Riding Centre (Area 13)
Rosie Lord, Berkshire Riding Centre Ltd, Crouch Lane, Windsor, Berkshire, SL4 4TN.
01344 884992
info@brc.uk.com

Bigland Hall Equine Group (Area 4)
Brow Edge, Haverthwaite, Ulverston, Cumbria, LA12 8PB.
01539 530333
bookings@biglandhall.com

Birr House Riding Centre (Area 17)
Caroline McVeigh, 81 Whinnery Hill, Craigantlet, Dundonald, Co Down, BT16 1UA.
02890 425858
carolinemcveigh@btinternet.com

Bishton Hall Riding School (Area 7)
Sarah Brown, St. Bedes Preparatory School, Bishton Hall, Stafford, Staffordshire, ST17 0XN.
01753 023053
bishtonponies@hotmail.co.uk

Blisworth Pony Club Centre (Area 12)
Kate Lee, New Tunnel Hill Farm, Stoke Road, Blisworth, Northamptonshire, NN7 3DB.
01604 858 041
katemadhouse@aol.com

Bourne Vale Riding Stables (Area 7)
Anna Cooper, Little Hardwick Road, Aldridge, Walsall, West Midlands, WS9 0SQ.
0121 353 7174
sales@bournevalestables.co.uk

Bourton Vale Equestrian Centre (Area 9)
Julia Petruzzelli, College Farm, Stow Road, Bourton-on-the-Water, Gloucestershire, GL54 2HN.
07910138465
office@bourtonvale.com

Bowdens Riding School at Balham (Area 15)
Annabelle Boucher, Balham Hill Farm, Chiselborough, South Petherton, Somerset, TA14 6TY.
07946 805696
info@bowdensridingschool.co.uk

Bowlers Riding School (Area 4)
Rachel Thomas, 35 Brewery Lane, Freshfield, Merseyside, L37 7DY.
01704 872915
bowlersridingschool@hotmail.com

Bowlings Riding School (Area 18)
Rebecca Haggar, Rudbaxton, Haverfordwest, Pembrokeshire, SA62 4DB.
01437 741407
bechaggar@aol.com

Bradbourne Riding and Training Centre (Area 11)
Teresa Watson, Bradbourne Vale Road, Sevenoaks, Kent, TN13 3DH.
01732 453592
bradbourneponyclub@gmail.com

Brampton Stables (Area 7)
, Stable Lane, Church Brampton, Northampton, Northamptonshire, NN6 8BH.
01604 842051
info@bramptonstables.com

Bridge End Equestrian (Area 3)
S-J Kendall, Bridge End Farm, Howe, Thirsk, North Yorkshire, YO7 4HT.
07866395028
sj@beequestrian.co.uk

Broadlands Riding Centre (Area 13)
Paige Parsons, Lower Paice Lane, Medstead, Alton, Hampshire, GU34 5PX.
01420375767
office@broadlandsgrouprda.org.uk

Brook Cottage Farm Riding School (Area 8)
Louise Seddon, Brook Cottage, Barley Croft End, Buntingford, Hertfordshire, SG9 0LL.
07919 888655
louise.seddon@btinternet.com

Broomhill Riding Centre (Area 1)
Broomhill Farm, Fortrose, Ross-shire, IV10 8SH.
01381 620214
lornanderson@hotmail.co.uk

Bryerley Springs Equestrian Centre (Area 12)
Ella Horner-Goss, Bryerley Springs Farm, Galley Lane, Milton Keynes, MK17 9AA.
01525 261823
admin@bryerleysprings.co.uk

Buckswood School Stables (Area 11)
Abbie Grove-Cook, Buckswood School, Rye Road, Guestling, East Sussex, TN35 4LT.
01424 813813
stables@buckswood.co.uk

Bulby Hall Equestrian Centre (Area 6)
Sue Bevan, Bulby Hall, Elsthorpe Road, Bulby, Bourne, Lincolnshire, PE10 0RU.
07483139232
susanfionabevan@outlook.com

Burley Villa School of Riding (Area 14)
Lisa Cremer, Bashley Common Road,
New Milton, Hampshire, BH25 5SH.
01425 610278
enquiry@burleyvilla.co.uk

Burnby Equestrian Centre (Area 3)
The Granary, Burnby Equestrian Centre, York,
Yorkshire, YO42 1RS.
07850 664992/ 07974506929
burnbyec@gmail.com

Burrows Lane Farm Riding School (Area 4)
Leanne Ryan, Burrows Lane, Eccleston,
Prescot, Merseyside, L34 6JQ.
07722251652
burrowslanefarm@live.co.uk

Bursted Hill Stables (Area 11)
Rebecca Tombs, Pett Bottom, Near Bridge,
Canterbury, Kent, CT4 6EH.
01227 830568
burstedhillstables@gmail.com

Cambridge and Newmarket Polo Academy (Area 8)
Victoria Lovatt, Frolic Farm, Lode Fen,
Cambridge, Cambridgeshire, CB25 9HF.
07740462024
rileyvj@hotmail.com

Cantref Pony Club Centre (Area 10)
Katherine Taylor, Upper Cantref Farm, Cantref,
Brecon, Powys, LD3 8LR.
01874 665223
riding@cantref.com

Cardiff Riding School (Area 10)
Clare Roberts, Pontcanna Fields, Llandaff,
Cardiff, CF5 2AX.
02920 383908
cardiffridingschool@cardiff.gov.uk

Casterton Sedbergh Prep School (Area 4)
Diane Hull, Kirkby Lonsdale, Carnforth,
Lancashire, LA6 2SG.
01524 279200
diane.hull@sedberghprep.org

Castle View Stables (Area 1)
Ashleigh Oldwick, Old Wick, Wick, Caithness,
Highlands, KW1 5TP.
07716 596164
ashleigholdwick@yahoo.co.uk

Cefngranod Stables (Area 18)
Dawn Hodson, Sarnau, Llandysul, Ceredigion,
SA44 6QB.
01239 654077
d.hodson@rocketmail.com

Cheshire Riding School (Area 5)
Debbie Wilson, Cogshall Lane, Comberbach,
Northwich, Cheshire, CW9 6BS.
01606 892111
info@cheshireridingschool.co.uk

Chestnut Farm Stables (Area 6)
Debi Varley, Chestnut Farm, Hallaton Road,
East Norton, Leicester, LE7 9XF.
01858 555822
brookam@hotmail.com

Church Farm Equestrian Centre (Area 14)
Church Farm Stables, Redlynch Lane, Bristol,
Somerset, BS31 2SL.
07787 561469
churchfarmec@outlook.com

Cimla Trekking and Equestrian Centre (Area 18)
Gilly Taylor, Hawdref Ganol, Cimla, Neath,
Glamorgan, SA12 9SL.
01639 644944
CimlaEquestrian@outlook.com

City of Derry Equestrian Centre (Area 17)
Pauline Lusby, 30 Bigwood Road, Ardmore, Derry, BT47 3RP.
07850 208656
info@cityofderryequestrian.com

Cliffhollins Riding School (Area 3)
Chelsea Gardner, Cliffhollins Lane, East Bierley, Bradford, Yorkshire, BD4 6RQ.
01274 651386
info@cliffhollins.co.uk

Clyne Farm Centre (Area 18)
Sarah Haden, Clyne Farm Centre, Westport Avenue, Mayals, Swansea, SA3 5AR.
01792 403333
hello@clynefarm.com

Coker Brown School of Riding (Area 16)
Charlotte Coker Brown, 14 Fairview Road, Denbury, Newton Abbot, Devon, TQ12 6ET.
07967 472097
charlottecoker-brown@hotmail.com

Coloured Cob Equestrian Centre (Area 6)
Sharon Tolley, Bank House Farm, Mansfield Road, Creswell, Nottinghamshire, S80 4AA.
01909 725251
sales@colouredcob.co.uk

Comeytrowe Equestrian Centre (Area 15)
Janet Neeld, Higher Comeytrowe Farm, Comeytrowe, Taunton, Somerset, TA4 1EQ.
01823 461385
equestrain@comeytrowe.co.uk

Conwy Community Riding Centre (Area 5)
Wendy Tobias-Jones, Tanrallt Farm, Henryd, Conwy, LL32 8EZ.
07840 871197
gwentj@btinternet.com

Corner Farm Equestrian (Area 7)
Lucy Johnson, Corner Farm Equestrian Centre, Painsbrook Lane, Shrewsbury, Shropshire, SY4 4BA.
01939 270944
lucy_k_johnson@hotmail.com

Cornilo Riding (Area 11)
Marina Aunger, The Stables, Sutton Court Farm, Sutton by Dover, Kent, CT15 5DF.
01304 380369
theoffice@corniloriding.com

Coton House Farm Stables (Area 7)
Helen Wakefield-Martin, Vicarage Lane, Whitington, Near Lichfield, Staffordshire, WS14 9LQ.
01543 432429
martindarr7@aol.com

Cotswold Polo Academy (Area 9)
Olivia Lamphee, Ewepens, The Park, Cirencester, Gloucestershire, GL7 6LY.
07900262405
olivia@oklequestrian.co.uk

Cotswold Riding (Area 9)
Pat Haine, Upper Woodhills Farm, Lower Lemington, Moreton-in-Marsh, Gloucestershire, GL56 9NW.
07508 773255
info@cotswoldriding.com

Cottagers Plot Equestrian Centre (Area 6)
Sophie Brown, Cottagers Plot, Laceby, Grimsby, Lincolnshire, DN37 7DX.
01472 276427
sophiebrown344@hotmail.com

Courses for Horses (Area 7)
Lower Stonehouse Farm, Brown Edge, Stoke on Trent, Staffordshire, ST6 8TF.
01782 505664
admin@coursesforhorses.org.uk

Coventry and District Pony Club (Area 7)
Sandy Sandon, Anker Cottage Farm, Caldecote, Nuneaton, Warwickshire, CV10 0TN.
02476383103
sandysandon@gmail.com

Croft Riding Centre Pony Club (Area 4)
Lynn Norton, Spring Lane, Croft, Warrington, Cheshire, WA3 7AS.
01925 763715
info@croftridingcentre.co.uk

Dark Deer Croft (Area 1)
Siobhan Thomson, Millness, Glen Urquhart, Inverness-shire, IV63 6TW.
01456 476201
info@darkdeer.co.uk

Darlington Stables (Area 5)
Hollymay Hickson, Hooter Hall, Elton Lane, Winterley, Cheshire, CW11 4TJ.
01270759319
darlington.stables@hotmail.com

Deandane Riding Stables (Area 4)
Martin Whalley, Gathurst Road, Shevington, Wigan, Lancashire, WN6 8JB.
01257 252855
deandane@btinternet.com

Deanswood Equestrian Centre (Area 8)
Sarah Dean, Cressing Park, Braintree Road, Cressing, Essex, CM77 8JB.
01376 560522
shareteam@hotmail.co.uk

Deepdene Riding Stables (Area 11)
Chelsea Donovan, Badlesmere, Ashford Road, Faversham, Kent, ME13 0NZ.
01233 740228
deepdenestables@gmail.com

Derrycrin Stables (Area 17)
Orlagh Oneill, Derrycrin Stables, 51 Derrycrin Road, Cookstown, County Tyrone, BT80 0HJ.
07874941900
derrycrinstables@hotmail.com

Dinefwr Riding Centre (Area 18)
Penny Jenner, Llandyfan, Ammanford, Carmarthenshire, SA18 2UD.
07989385785
info@beaconsequestrian.com

Dittiscombe Equestrian Centre (Area 16)
Alex Farleigh, Slapton, Kingsbridge, Devon, TQ7 2QF.
01548 581049
alex.farleigh1@btinternet.com

Dorset Polo Club (Area 14)
Robert Brockett, Lytchett Heath Farm, Huntick Road, Poole, BH16 6BB.
01202 623985
office@dorsetpolo.co.uk

Dovecote Farm Equestrian Centre (Area 6)
Heather Gunn, Dovecote Farm, Orston, Nottinghamshire, NG13 9NS.
01949 851204
dovecotefarm@hotmail.com

Ealing Riding School (Area 12)
Louise Saunders, 17-19 Gunnersbury Avenue, London, W5 3XD.
02089923808
admin@ealingridingschool.net

Ebony Horse Club (Area 11)
Tom Warmerdam, Ebony Horse Club, 51 Millbrook Road, Brixton, SW9 7JD.
02077383478
info@ebonyhorseclub.org

Eccleston Equestrian Centre (Area 4)
Kayleigh Browne, Ulnes Walton Lane, Leyland, Preston, Lancashire, PR26 8LT.
01772 600093
karen@equestrian-northwest.co.uk

Echos Equestrian (Area 12)
Lauren Dawes, Slough Road, Iver Heath, Buckinghamshire, SL0 0DZ.
01895 347186
lauren@echosequestrian.co.uk

Equestrian at Coworth Park (Area 13)
Gemma Porter-Rawlings, Coworth Park Hotel, Blacknest Road, Sunninghill, Ascot, Berkshire, SL5 7SE.
01344 756763 / 07584
equestrian.cpa@dorchestercollection.com

Equine Learning (Area 7)
Nicola Hepburn, Wootton Park Farm, Alcester Road, Wootton Wawen, Henley in Arden, Warwickshire, B95 6HJ.
01564 642101
hello@equinelearning.org.uk

Eston Equitation Centre (Area 2)
Laura Storey, Villa Marie, Occupation Road, Eston, Middlesbrough, Cleveland, TS6 9HA.
01642 452260
Estonequitationcentre@gmail.com

Evergreen Stables (Area 12)
Rachel Billing, Billings Brook Farm, Wrights Lane, Gayton, Northamptonshire, NN7 3ES.
01604 858247
billingsbrookstables@gmail.com

Faughanvale Stables (Area 17)
Patricia Dalton, 11 Dunlade Road, Greysteel, Co Derry, BT47 3EF.
02871 811843
valestables@hotmail.co.uk

Fergushill Riding Stables (Area 19)
Gillian Beattie, Broomhill Farm, Fergushill, Kilwinning, Ayrshire, KA13 7RF.
07842 166799
cevara@btinternet.com

Field House Equestrian Centre (Area 2)
Rebekah Reay, Fieldhouse Farm, Howden Le Wear, Crook, Durham, DL15 8EE.
01388 766687
rebekahreay@live.co.uk

Finchale View Riding School (Area 2)
Lauren Craggs, Pitt House Lane, Leamside, County Durham, DH4 6QR.
07761 642435
finchaleview@gmail.com

Fletchers Farm Riding School (Area 8)
Helen Hill, Fletchers Farm, Rams Farm Road, Fordham, Colchester, Essex, CO6 3NT.
01206 242210
manager@fletchersfarm.co.uk

Folly Farm Equestrian Centre (Area 6)
Rebecca Hardy, 25 London Road, Yaxley, Peterborough, Cambs, PE7 3NQ.
01733 242783
follyfarmequestrian@yahoo.co.uk

Fordbank Equestrian Centre (Area 19)
Fiona Ferguson, Fairydale Cottage, Beith Road, Johnstone, PA10 2NS.
07572 424692
feefee42@live.co.uk

Fort Widley Equestrian Centre (Area 13)
Jodie Thackeray, Portsdown Hill Road, Cosham, Portsmouth, Hampshire, PO6 3LS.
02392 324553
equestrian@peterashleyactivitycentres.co.uk

Foxcote House Riding School (Area 9)
Sarah Everitt, Foxcote House, Foxcote, Cheltenham, GL54 4LW.
01242 820663
sarah.everitt@live.com

Foxhills Riding Centre (Area 7)
David Blake, Beacon Dairy Farm, Doe Bank Lane, Walsall, West Midlands, WS9 0RQ.
01213 609160
info@mygg.co.uk

Free Spirit Equestrian (Area 17)
Lorraine Hutchinson, 41 Maytown Road, Bessbrook, Newry, Co Down, BT35 7NE.
07775 724667
freespiritequestrian@gmail.com

Friars Hill Stables (Area 3)
Alison Brown, Friars Hill, Sinnington, York, Yorkshire, YO62 6SL.
01751 432758
friarshillridingstables@gmail.com

Ghyll Park Equestrian (Area 11)
Sally-Ann Dale, Little Trodgers, Lake Street, Crowborough, East Sussex, TN6 3NT.
07974638536
sally@ghyllparkequestrian.co.uk

Gillians Riding School Pony Club Centre (Area 8)
Brayside Farm, Clay Hill, Enfield, Middlesex, EN2 9JL.
020 8366 5445
gilliansridingschool@outlook.com

Glapthorn Manor Equestrian (Area 6)
Charlotte Dorner, Glapthorn Manor, Glapthorn, Peterborough, PE8 5BJ.
07778521413
glapthornstables@outlook.com

Glen Tanar Equestrian Centre (Area 1)
Sheena Thomson, Glen Tanar Equestrian Centre, Glen Tanar, Aboyne, Aberdeenshire, AB34 5EU.
01339 886448
Sheena431@icloud.com

Gleneagles Equestrian Centre (Area 1)
Rebecca Kennedy, The Equestrian School, The Gleneagles Hotel, Auchterarder, Perthshire, PH3 1NF.
01764 694344
equestrian@gleneagles.com

Gleneagles Equestrian Centre (Area 13)
Lucy Nicosia, Allington Lane, West End, Southampton, Hampshire, SO30 3HQ.
02380 473370 / 07796
info@gleneagles.org.uk

Grafton Farm Riding Centre Ltd (Area 7)
Sue Thomas, Bockleton, Tenbury Wells, Worcestershire, WR15 8PT.
01568 750602
grafton.farm@btinternet.com

Grassroots (Area 11)
Fiona House, Church Farm, Crowhurst Lane, Lingfield, Surrey, RH7 6LR.
07498551262
fiona@withgrassroots.co.uk

Great Trethew Trekking (Area 16)
Elizabeth Walke, Great Trethew Farm, Horningtops, Liskeard, Cornwall, PL14 3PY.
07714099127
greattrethewtrekking@gmail.com

Greatham Equestrian Centre (Area 13)
Crystal Roche, Springwood Stables, Longmoor Road, Greatham, Hampshire, GU33 6AH.
01420 538810
info@greathamequestriancentre.co.uk

Green Farm Riding Stables (Area 18)
Zana Llewellyn, The Green, Trebanos, Pontardawe, Swansea, West Glamorgan, SA8 4BR.
01792 862947
l.zana@yahoo.co.uk

Green Meadow Riding Centre (Area 10)
Judith England, Dare Valley Country Park, Aberdare, Mid-Glamorgan, CF44 7PT.
01685 874961
judith.england@btconnect.com

Greenways Stables Ltd (Area 13)
Sally Blackmore (13), Lower Eashing, Godalming, Surrey, GU7 2QF.
07442530080
info@greenways-stables.co.uk

Grenoside Equestrian Centre Ltd (Area 3)
Zoe Smith, Barnes Green, Penistone Road, Grenoside, Sheffield, South Yorkshire, S35 8NA.
01142 402548
hello@grenoside-equestrian.co.uk

Grove Farm Riding School (Area 11)
Jess Cruwys, Grove Lane, Iden, Nr Rye, East Sussex, TN31 7PX.
07760126145
grovefarm.rs@hotmail.co.uk

Grove House Stables Pony Club Centre (Area 6)
Andrew Stennett, Grovewood Road, Misterton, Doncaster, South Yorkshire, DN10 4EF.
01427 890802
ghs1991@grovehousestables.co.uk

Gym-Khana (Area 8)
Phoebe Ling, Valley Farm Equestrian Leisure, Valley Farm, Woodbridge, Suffolk, IP13 0ND.
01728 746916
phoebe@valleyfarm.co.uk

Hall Farm Stables (Area 8)
Tessa Frost, Cambridge Road, Waterbeach, Cambridgeshire, CB25 9NJ.
01223 860087
enquiries@hallfarmstables.com

Hanford School (Area 14)
Charlotte Pearson, Hanford School, Child Okeford, Blandford Forum, DT11 8HN.
01258 860219
pearsonc@hanfordschool.co.uk

Hargate Equestrian (Area 6)
Chloe Davis, Egginton Road, Hilton, Derbyshire, DE65 5FJ.
01283 734981
hargateequestrian@yahoo.co.uk

Havard Stables (Area 18)
Hannah McLoughlin, Havard Stables, Dinas Cross, Newport, Pembrokeshire, SA42 0SR.
07968 647762
havardstables@live.co.uk

Hayfield EC (Area 1)
Caroline Martin, Hazelhead Park, Aberdeen, Aberdeenshire, AB15 8BB.
01224 315703
info@hayfield.com

Hemsted Forest Equestrian Centre (Area 11)
Kerry Hobbs, Golford Road, Benenden, Kent, TN17 4AJ.
01580 240086
hemstedforestec@gmail.com

Hertfordshire Polo Academy (Area 8)
Alec Banner Eve, Hertfordshire Polo Academy, Millfield Lane, Ware, Hertfordshire, SG11 2ED.
07736060200
team@mhfpolo.com

Hewshott Farm Stables (Area 13)
Caroline Ewen, Hewshott Lane, Liphook, Hants, GU30 7SU.
07721 650758
info@hewshottfarmstables.co.uk

Hill Farm Equestrian Centre (8) (Area 8)
Hazel Ackland, Stonewold, Hill Farm Lane, Chelmondiston, Suffolk, IP9 1JU.
01473 780406
hillfarmec@hotmail.co.uk

Hill Farm Riding Stables and Pony Club Centre (Area 13)
Jayne Brown, Hill Lane, Freshwater, Isle of Wight, PO40 9TQ.
07748 253899
hillfarmstablesiow@gmail.com

Hill Farm Stables (Elmswell) (Area 8)
Sarah Moorbey, Ashfields Road, Elmswell, Suffolk, IP30 9HL.
07845 320424
hillfarmridingschool@yahoo.com

Hilltop Equestrian Centre (Area 8)
Ann Malone, 180 High Street, Yelling, Cambridgeshire, PE19 6SD.
01480 880232
ann@mariemalone.plus.com

Hole Farm Trekking Centre (Area 7)
Amelia Woolley, 36 Watery Lane, Quinton, Birmingham, West Midlands, B32 3BS.
0121 422 3464
cjones60@sky.com

Holly Riding School (Area 7)
Nicky Pritchard, Hurley Common, Atherstone, Warwickshire, CV9 2LR.
01827 872205
nickypritchard16@aol.com

Holt's Equestrian Centre (Area 4)
Anne-Margaret Holt, Dry Gap Farm, Bury Old Road, Bury, BL0 0RX.
07717527399
holt-equestrian@hotmail.co.uk

Hooks Cross Equestrian (Area 8)
Ruth Collins, Oaks Cross Farm, Hooks Cross, Watton-at-Stone, Hertfordshire, SG14 3RY.
01920 438240
hookscrossequestrian@gmail.com

Horse Riding Cornwall @Poldice (Area 16)
Karen Trezise, Poldice Valley Equine & Events Arena, Carharrack, Redruth, Cornwall, TR16 5RB.
07756662959
Horseridingcornwall@outlook.com

Hot to Trot School of Equitation (Area 8)
Hannah Wright, 148 Bunwell Street, Bunwell, Norwich, Norfolk, NR16 1QY.
07738 615775
info@hottotrotschoolofequitation.co.uk

Hundleby Riding Centre (Area 6)
Sian Lovatt, Sumpter Farm, North Beck Lane, Hundleby, Lincolnshire, PE23 5NB.
07584 047340
slequinejournalism@gmail.com

Huntersfield Equestrian Centre (Area 9)
Nico Van den Berg, Petwick Farm, Challow, Faringdon, Oxfordshire, SN7 8NT.
07729 680573
nico@huntersfieldec.com

Hunterswood Riding and Livery Stables (Area 16)
Christine Weeks, Yeoford, Crediton, Devon, EX17 5ET.
01363 772594
c.c.weeks@icloud.com

Inadown Farm Livery Stables (Area 13)
Rachel Chubb, Newton Valence, Alton, Hampshire, GU34 3RR.
01420 588439
inadown@yahoo.co.uk

Island Riding Centre (Area 13)
Louise Buckner, Staplers Road, Newport, Isle of Wight, PO30 2NB.
01983214000
louise@islandriding.com

K A Horses (Area 7)
Kerry Davies, The Lake House, Turley Green, Bridgnorth, Shropshire, WV15 6LR.
07919 484727
enquiries@kahorses.co.uk

Keysoe International Pony Club Centre (Area 12)
Frances Murray, Church Road, Bedford, Bedfordshire, MK44 2JP.
07944987134
info@keysoetherapycentre.com

Kiln Stables Riding School (Area 13)
Angela Macleod, The Old Kiln Farm, Farnham Road, Farnham, GU10 4JZ.
01420 520005
angelajandrew@aol.com

Kilnsey Trekking and Riding Centre (Area 4)
Michelle Parkin-Vaughan, The Homestead, Conistone with Kilnsey, Skipton, Yorkshire, BD23 5HS.
01756 752861
janepighills@btinternet.com

Kimblewick Equestrian Centre (Area 8)
Nikkita Gostling, Low Road, North Tuddenham, Dereham, Norfolk, NR20 3HF.
07856 266990
nikkita@kimblewick.co.uk

Kingsmead Equestrian Centre (Area 11)
Fiona Tothill, Kingswood Lane, Hamsey Green, Warlingham, Surrey, CR6 9AB.
0208 657 0832
enquiries@kingsmeadec.co.uk

La Rocco Riding School (Area 16)
Lisa Dubois, Pennybrook Farm, Lower Newlands, Bradworthy, Devon, EX22 7RN.
01409 240166
ssalisbury462@btinternet.com

Lacys Cottage Riding School (Area 3)
Nichola Pimlott, Scrayingham, York, Yorkshire, YO41 1JD.
01759 371586
nicholapimlott@icloud.com

Lakefield Equestrian Centre (Area 16)
Becky Monk, Lower Pendavey Farm, Camelford, Cornwall, PL32 9TX.
01840 213279
lakefieldequestriancentre@btconnect.com

Landlords Farm Equestrian Centre (Area 4)
Michelle Pendlebury, Dicconson Lane, Aspull, Wigan, Lancashire, WN2 1QD.
01942 831329
michellependlebury@hotmail.co.uk

Lands End Equestrian Centre (Area 13)
Suzy Jones, Whistley Mill Lane, Twyford, Reading, Berkshire, RG10 0RA.
07834 838111
info@landsendec.com

Langtoft Stables (Area 6)
Carolyne Lister, Langtoft Fen, Peterborough, Cambridgeshire, PE6 9NX.
07703 743159
langstables@hotmail.co.uk

Larkrigg Riding School (Area 4)
Anne Wilson, Natland, Nr Kendal, Cumbria, LA9 7QS.
01539 560245
larkrigg@hotmail.co.uk

Laurel View Equestrian Centre (Area 17)
Laurel Faloona, 18 Knowehead Road, Templepatrick, Ballyclare, Co Antrim, BT39 0BX.
02890 830649
laurelview01@btinternet.com

Lee Valley Riding Centre (Area 8)
Nicole Cox, 71 Leabridge Road, Leyton, London, E10 7QL.
020 8556 2629
nicole.cox@gll.org

Liege Manor Equestrian (Area 10)
Georgia Basett, Liege Manor, Bonvilston, Vale of Glamorgan, CF5 6TQ.
01446 781648
liegemanor@btconnect.com

Little Brook Equestrian (Area 11)
Sally O'Neill, East Park Lane, Newchapel, Near Lingfield, Surrey, RH7 6HS.
01342 837546
sally@littlebrookequestrian.co.uk

Little Margate Equestrian (Area 16)
Rachel Philpott, Little Margate Farm, Margate Lane, Bodmin, Cornwall, PL30 4AL.
07917 762102
info@littlemargateequestrian.com

Little Wratting Riding School at Cooks Farm (Area 8)
Tayla Trowbridge, Cooks Farm, Hartest, Bury St. Edmunds, Suffolk, IP29 4DZ.
07507647188
taylatrowbridge@btinternet.com

Littlebourne Equestrian Centre (Area 12)
Ben Mitchell Winter, Littlebourne Farm, Northwood Road, Harefield, Middlesex, UB9 6PU.
01895 824350
ben@littlebournefarm.co.uk

Lodge Equine Stables (Area 17)
Lesley Johnston, 10 Ballyloughan Road, Richhill, Co Armagh, BT61 9ND.
02838 870359
lesleyjohnston20@gmail.com

Lodge Farm Equestrian Centre (Area 7)
Debbie Machin, Off Mill Lane, Wetley Rocks, Stoke on Trent, Staffordshire, ST9 0BN.
01782 551961
info@lodgefarmriding.co.uk

Lodge Riding Centre (Area 4)
Debbie King, Dacres Bridge Lane, Tarbock, Merseyside, L35 1QZ.
0151 489 8886
orry.king@btinternet.com

Long Lane Equestrian (Area 6)
23 Bridge Fields, Kegworth, Derby, Leicestershire, DE74 2FW.
01509 674655
longlane.equestrian@hotmail.com

Longdole Polo Academy (Area 9)
Lorna Broughton, Longdole Farm, Birdlip, Gloucester, Gloucestershire, GL4 8LH.
07917833853
academy@longdolepolo.com

Longfield Equestrian Centre (Area 4)
Kate Farmer, Middle Longfield Farm, Long Hey Lane, Todmorden, Lancashire, OL14 6JN.
01706 812736
info@longfieldequestriancentre.co.uk

Lower Tokenbury Equestrian Centre (Area 16)
Roslyn Lucas, Lower Tokenbury Farm, Upton Cross, Liskeard, Cornwall, PL14 5AR.
07880 702704
tokenburyriding@hotmail.co.uk

Luccombe Riding Centre (Area 14)
Terri Cook, Luccombe Farm, Milton Abbas, Blandford Forum, DT11 0BD.
07585392234
luccomberidingcentre@gmail.com

Lucton School (Area 10)
Emma Coates, Lucton School, Lucton, Leominster, Herefordshire, HR6 9PN.
01568 782000
office@luctonschool.org

Lychgate Farm Equestrian LLP (Area 7)
Jane Brown, Lychgate Lane, Hinckley, Leicestershire, LE10 2DS.
01455 632188
lychgatefarm@gmail.com

Malvern Riding School (Area 9)
Julie Davies-Bennetts, Northend Farm House, Northend Lane, Malvern, Worcestershire, WR13 5AD.
07766 853668
handsonhorses@btinternet.com

Mannix Equestrian Centre (Area 11)
Jackie Goddard, Nightingale Farm, Whiteacre Lane, Waltham, Near Canterbury, Kent, CT4 5SR.
07896671966
jackie@mannixequestriancentre.co.uk

Midgeland Riding School (Area 4)
Joanna Dobson, 460 Midgeland Road, Marton Moss, Blackpool, Lancashire, FY4 5EE.
01253 693312
midgeland@hotmail.co.uk

Mierscourt Valley Riding School (Area 11)
Robert Vallance, Mierscourt Road, Rainham, Gillingham, Kent, ME8 8PH.
07736 454388
mierscourtvalleyrs@gmail.com

Mill House (Area 6)
Anna Walker, Mill Lane, Belton, Loughborough, Leicestershire, LE12 9UJ.
07968 118850
annacbaxter@aol.com

Moat Farm Riding Centre (Area 8)
Patricia Adams, Moat Farm, Golden Lane, Lawshall, Bury St Edmunds, Suffolk, IP29 4PS.
01284 830098
tish@moat-farm.co.uk

Moor Farm Stables (Area 7)
Tiffany Hill, Wall Hill Road, Corley Moor, Coventry, Warwickshire, CV7 8AP.
01676 540594
liz@mfstables.co.uk

Moorview Equestrian Centre (Area 4)
Ursula Dalton, Blacksnape Road, Blacksnape, Darwen, Lancashire, BB3 3PP.
01254 701557
moorviewreception@yahoo.co.uk

Mount Mascal Stables (Area 11)
Alison Window, Vicarage Road, Bexley, Kent, DA5 2AW.
020 8300 3947
ali@mountmascalstables.com

Murton Equestrian Centre (Area 2)
Leigh Belbin, The Bridle, Murton Village, Shiremoor, Newcastle upon Tyne, Northumberland, NE27 0QD.
0191 257 1369
murtonequestriancentre@gmail.com

Mutterton Equine (Area 15)
Jo Palmer, Mutterton Cottage, Cullompton, Devon, EX15 1RL.
07795 664498
canadawooduk@gmail.com

Myddelton College (Area 5)
Katy Powell, Myddleton College, Castle Ward House, Denbigh, Denbighshire, LL16 3EN.
01745 472201
Office@myddeltoncollege.com

Naburn Grange Riding Centre (Area 3)
Briony Horn, York Road, Naburn, York, North Yorkshire, YO19 4RU.
01904 728283
brionyh10@hotmail.com

Nelson Park Riding Centre (Area 11)
Sarah Catterall, St Margarets Road, Woodchurch, Birchington, Kent, CT7 0HJ.
01843 822251
nelsonparkridingcentre@googlemail.com

New Direction (Area 6)
Hannah Oliver, Ringer Lane, Clowne, Derbyshire, S43 4BX.
01246 810456
hannah@new-direction.org.uk

New Hill House (Area 4)
Danielle Perez, New Hill House Farm, Wood Lane, Great Altcar, Lancashire, L37 9BQ.
07590 455404
danielleperez@hotmail.co.uk

Newark Equestrian (Area 6)
Rachel Foster, Coddington Lane, Balderton, Newark, Nottinghamshire, NG24 3NB.
07714 182876
refoster19@gmail.com

Newton Ferrers Equus (Area 16)
Leah Harris, Newton Downs Farm, Newton Ferrers, Devon, PL8 1JA.
01752 872 807
leahfoxharris@gmail.com

NMW Riding Academy (Area 1)
Rachael Doubleday, Orcadia, Keith Hall, Inverurie, Aberdeenshire, AB51 0LL.
07883081295
Info@nmwridingacademy.co.uk

Noakes Farm Riding Centre (Area 9)
Sallie Barrett, Bredenbury, Bromyard, Herefordshire, HR7 4SY.
01885 483467
noakesfarm@btconnect.com

Northampton High School Pony Club (Area 12)
Karla Hodgetts-Tate, Newport Pagnell Road, Northampton, NN4 6UU.
01604 765765
k.hodgetts-tate@nhs.gdst.net

Northington Stud and Stables (Area 13)
Francesca Baring, Grange Park, Northington Road, Alresford, SO24 9TG.
07970 717093
northingtonstudandstables@gmail.com

NTC Pony Club (Area 7)
Charlotte Williams, Lowlands Farm, Old Warwick Road, Warwick, Warwickshire, CV35 7AX.
01926843403
cw.lowlands@rda.org.uk

Nuneaton and North Warwickshire Equestrian Centre (Area 7)
Sue Lynch, Valley Road, Galley Common, Nuneaton, Warwickshire, CV10 9NJ.
02476 392397

info@nnwec.org.uk

Oakfield Farm Pony Club Centre (Area 6)
Amanda Wain, Belper Road, Stanley Common, Ilkeston, Derbyshire, DE7 6FP.
01159 305358
shaunwain3090@gmail.com

Oakhanger Riding and Pony Club Centre (Area 5)
Natalie Ecclestone, Holmshaw Lane, Crewe, Cheshire, CW1 5XE.
01270 876311
oakhangerridingcentre@outlook.com

Oaklands Riding School (Area 15)
Jacky Newbery, Oaklands, Ball Farm Road, Alphington, Exeter, Devon, EX2 9JA.
01392 272105
jacky@newoakstud.co.uk

Oakview Stables (Area 8)
Charlotte Rule, Oak View Farm, Lowestoft Road, Great Yarmouth, Norfolk, NR31 9BD.
07825 986906
darcy1982@hotmail.co.uk

Offchurch Bury Polo Club (Area 7)
Tessa Collett, The Offchurch Bury Estate, Offchurch Bury, Leamington Spa, Warwickshire, CV33 9AR.
07816 830887 / 07901803285
tessa@offchurchburypoloclub.co.uk

Old Bexley Stables Pony Club (Area 11)
Wendy Tucker, Stable Lane, Vicarage Road, Bexley, Kent, DA5 2AW.
01322 557745
oldbex@aol.com

Old Mill Stables (Area 16)
Jade Booton, Old Mill Stables, Lelant Downs, Hayle, Cornwall, TR27 6LN.
01736 753045
oldmillenquiries@gmail.com

Old Tiger Stables at North Angle Farm (Area 8)
Hayley James, North Angle Farm, Angle Common, Ely, Cambridgeshire, CB7 5HX.
07410438840
oldtigerstables@outlook.com

Oldmoor Farm Riding School (Area 6)
Katie Renn, Oldmoor Farm, Robinettes Lane, Babbington, Nottinghamshire, NG16 2ST.
07729 529042
oldmoorfarmridingschool@sky.com

Otterbourne Riding Centre (Area 14)
Sarah Jackson, Rue de Planel, Torteval, Guernsey, GY8 0LX.
01481 263085
nicholas_jackson@hotmail.co.uk

Oxford Polo (Area 12)
David Ashby, Kemsley Farm, Akeman Street, Bicester, Oxfordshire, OX25 3AA.
07989389130
info@oxfordpolo.co.uk

Oxmardyke Equestrian Centre (Area 3)
Rachel Kirby, Field View House, Tongue Lane, Gilberdyke, East Yorkshire, HU15 2UY.
07961 104690
oecuk@outlook.com

P and R Equestrian Centre (Area 6)
Pearl Massey, The Paddocks, Claxy Bank, Friskney, Boston, PE22 8PN.
07545 813962
pearlmasseyis@aol.com

Park Farm Riding School (Area 11)
Anne Seymour, Park Road, Preston, Canterbury, Kent, CT3 1HD.
01227 728349
parkfarmriding@yahoo.co.uk

Park Hall Equestrian (Area 8)
Penny Townsend, Park Hall Farm,
Park Hall Road, Somersham, Huntingdon,
Cambridgeshire, PE28 3HQ.
07594 449583
penny_townsend22@yahoo.co.uk

Park Lane Stables (Area 11)
Natalie O'Rourke, Park Lane Stables,
Petersham Road, Richmond, TW10 7AH.
07796842328
theteam@parklanestables.co.uk

Park Palace Ponies (Area 4)
Bridget Griffin, Park Palace Ponies, 253
Mill Street, Liverpool, Merseyside, L8 6QN.
01517080624
parkpalaceponies@gmail.com

Parklands Arena (Area 6)
Ruth Sampson, Parklands, Worksop Road,
Aston, Sheffield, Yorkshire, S26 2AD.
07798 700733
sampsonruth@gmail.com

Parkside Stables (Area 6)
Amanda Stalker, Wingfield Road, Alfreton,
Derbyshire, DE55 7AP.
01773 835193
info@parksidestables.co.uk

Parkview Riding School (Area 6)
Charlie McDonald, 100 Ansty Lane, Thurcaston,
Leicestershire, LE7 7JB.
0116 236 4858
charlie@parkviewridingschool.co.uk

Pathhead Equestrian Centre (Area 1)
Ali Caldow, Pathhead Farm, Forfar Road,
Kirriemuir, Angus, DD8 5BY.
01575 572173
enquiries@pathhead.com

Pen Y Coed Riding Stables (Area 5)
George Hanson, Llynclys Hill, Oswestry,
Shropshire, SY10 8LG.
01691 830608
penycoedridingstables@outlook.com

Petasfield Stables (Area 8)
Crissie Flemming, Mangrove Lane, Hertford,
Hertfordshire, SG13 8QQ.
07775 931343
crissie@petasfieldstables.com

Pevlings Farm Riding and Livery Stables (Area 14)
Alison Tytheridge, Cabbage Lane, Horsington,
Templecombe, Somerset, BA8 0DA.
01963 370990
atytheridge@hotmail.co.uk

Pigeon House Equestrian (Area 9)
Sarah Hill, Pigeon House Lane,
Church Hanborough, Witney, Oxfordshire,
OX29 8AF.
01993 881628
schill2005@icloud.com

Pine Ridge Riding School (Area 11)
Jenny Butler-Smith, Pound Lane, Knockholt,
Kent, TN14 7NE.
01959 533161
pineridgers@hotmail.com

Polwhele House Riding School (Area 16)
Miriam Hopper, Polwhele House School,
Polwhele, Truro, Cornwall, TR4 9AE.
riding@polwhelehouse.co.uk

Pony Grove (Area 13)
Karen Sinclair-Williams, The Chalet,
Ruxbury Road, Chertsey, Surrey, KT16 9NJ.
07802766423
ponygrovelimited@gmail.com

Priory Place Equestrian (Area 8)
Joely Parradine, Priory Place, Grange Lane, Dunmow, Essex, CM6 3HY.
07879335545
Prioryplace.ec@outlook.com

Putley Pony Club Centre (Area 9)
Jean Buttle, Newtons Farm, Putley, Ledbury, Herefordshire, HR8 2QW.
01531 670256
putleyhorseridingschool@outlook.com

Quarry Farm Riding Stables (Area 11)
Rosie Langbridge, Quarry Farm, West Park Road, Lingfield, Surrey, RH7 6HT.
07710 681494
officequarryfarm@gmail.com

Queen Mary's Equestrian Centre (Area 3)
Alice Clennan, Queen Marys School, Baldersby Park, Thirsk, North Yorkshire, YO7 3BZ.
01845575000
riding@queenmarys.org

Radway Equestrian (Area 7)
Jane Holdsworth, Rectory Farm, Epwell, Banbury, Oxfordshire, OX15 6LR.
01295 670265
radwayequestrian@gmail.com

Raw Equine (Area 6)
Jodie Eyre, The Gallops, Dozens Bank, Spalding, Lincolnshire, PE11 3ND.
jodiehoward_5@hotmail.co.uk

Rawreth Equestrian Centre (Area 8)
Laura Jack, Rawreth Equestrian Centre, Old Burrells, Church Road, Wickford, Essex, SS11 8SH.
01268 732227
rawrethec@gmail.com

RD Equestrian (Area 17)
Roisin Donnelly, 126 Main Street, Fintona, Co. Tyrone, BT78 2AE.
07709 846447
rd10@hotmail.co.uk

REACH (Area 8)
Louise Lees, R E A C H, Crown Farm Stables, Crown Road, Brentwood, Essex, CM14 5TB.
07519169913
Reach.hippotherapy@gmail.com

Red Park Equestrian Centre (Area 15)
Jill Martin, Egrove Way, Williton, Somerset, TA4 4TB.
01984 632373
red.park@btinternet.com

Red Piece Equestrian Stables (Area 6)
Antonia McKinnon-Wood, Stanion Road, Brigstock, Northamptonshire, NN14 1DZ.
07854 323626
redpiecees@gmail.com

Regal Equestrian (Area 9)
John Bird, Green Lane Farm, Green Lane, Shipston-on-Stour, Warwickshire, CV36 5BL.
01608 684113
admin@regalequestrian.co.uk

Rheidol Riding Centre (Area 18)
Iola Evans, Capel Bangor, Aberystwyth, Ceredigion, SY23 4EL.
01970 880863
iola.evans@btinternet.com

Ridge Farm Riding School (Area 11)
Fiona McGuinness, Ridge Farm Cottage, Ridge Row, Acrise, Near Folkestone, Kent, CT18 8JT.
07866001273
ridgefarmridingschool@gmail.com

Riverside Equestrian Centre (Area 3)
Michaela Preston, Heron Bank Farm, Bawtry Road, Tickhill, Doncaster, Yorkshire, DN11 9EX.
01302 744499
riversideeqc@btinternet.com

Rockstar Equine (Area 7)
Kay Scott-Jarvis, Cocksparrow Lane, Penkridge, Staffordshire, WS12 4PB.
01543406021
kay.rockstarequitationcentre@gmail.com

Roman Bank Equestrian (Area 8)
Coral Herbert, Roman Bank, Walpole St Andrew, Near Wisbech, Cambridgeshire, PE14 7JY.
01945 780179
rbepc@hotmail.com

Roocroft Riding Stables (Area 4)
Judith Burton, Barrons Farm, Courage Low Lane, Wrightington, Nr Wigan, Lancashire, WN6 9PJ.
01257 252225
judith_burton@hotmail.com

Rookery Team Pony Club (Area 7)
Natalie Burrows, Rookery Farm, Ettington, Stratford on Avon, Warwickshire, CV37 7TN.
07973 133569
rookeryteampcc@gmail.com

Rookin House Farm (Area 2)
Shelley Fell, Troutbeck, Penrith, Cumberland, CA11 0SS.
01768 483561
enquiries@rookinhouse.co.uk

Rosewall Equestrian (Area 14)
Mary Green, Mills Road, Osmington Mills, Weymouth, Dorset, DT3 6HA.
01305 833578
riding@weymouthcamping.com

Royal Alexandra and Albert School (Area 11)
Pamela Penston, Gatton park, Reigate, Surrey, RH2 0TD.
01737 649069
stables@gatton-park.org.uk

Royal Armoured Corps Saddle Club (Area 14)
Sue Cobb, RAC Saddle Club Office, Allenby Barracks, Wareham, BH20 6JA.
01929 403 580
office@racsaddleclub.co.uk

Russells Equestrian Centre (Area 13)
Verity Tidmarsh, Russell Equestrian Centre, New Place, Allington Lane, Southampton, Hampshire, SO30 3HQ.
02380 473693
veritytidmarsh@yahoo.co.uk

Rye Street Farm Equestrian Centre (Area 11)
Hannah Loveridge, Rye Street, Cliffe, Rochester, Kent, ME3 7UD.
01634 221030
rye.street@btinternet.com

S J Equestrian (Area 3)
Silvia Schuler, Farm View Hall, Warsill, Harrogate, HG3 3LH.
07900 692250
silvia@bewerleyriding.com

Saddles Riding Centre (Area 11)
Carly Thomas, Stable Lane, Off Vicarage Road, Bexley, Kent, DA5 2AW.
07854 610820
saddlesrc@gmail.com

Sandridgebury Riding School (Area 12)
Kirby Halling, Sandridgebury Farm, Sandridgebury Lane, St. Albans, Hertfordshire, AL3 6JB.
01727 851952

office@sandridgeburyridingschool.co.uk

Sandroyd School (Area 14)
Harriet Wates, Sandroyd School, Rushmore Park, Salisbury, Wiltshire, SP5 5QD.
01725 516264
hwates@sandroyd.com

Sawston Riding School (Area 8)
Sarah Maddison, Sawston Riding School, Common Lane, Cambridge, Cambridgeshire, CB22 3HW.
01223 835198
sawstonridingschool@live.co.uk

Scholland Equestrian at Kilconquhar (Area 1)
Debbie Maas, Kilconquhar Castle, Kilconquher, Leven, Fife, KY9 IEZ.
01333 340501
info@scholland.com

Seaview Riding School (Area 4)
Claire Hayton, Biggar Village, Walney Island, Barrow in Furness, Cumbria, LA14 3YG.
01229 474251
claireseaview@hotmail.co.uk

Severnvale Equestrian Centre (Area 10)
Debbie Wilding, Tidenham, Chepstow, Monmouthshire, NP16 7LL.
01291 623412
svec@clara.co.uk

Shardeloes Farm Equestrian Centre (Area 12)
Tracey Lyon, Cherry Lane, Woodrow, Amersham, Buckinghamshire, HP7 0QF.
01494 433333
office@shardeloesfarm.com

Shedfield Equestrian Centre (Area 13)
Mollie Mullen, Shedfield Equestrian Centre, Botley Road, Southampton, Hampshire, SO32 2HL.
01329 830387
shedfielderidingschool@gmail.com

Shrivenham Equestrian Centre (Area 9)
Beccy Allan, Shrivenham Equestrian Centre, Shrivenham, Swindon, Wiltshire, SN6 8LA.
01793 785489
enquiries@shrivenhamsaddleclub.co.uk

Silvermere Equestrian Centre (Area 13)
Beth Bradbury, Bramley Hedge Farm, Redhill Road, Cobham, Surrey, KT11 1EQ.
01932 864040
enquiries@silvermere-equestrian.co.uk

Silverstone Riding Stables (Area 12)
Sophie Brennan, Blackmires Farm, Silverstone, Towcester, Northamptonshire, NN12 8UZ.
01327 857280
silverstoneriding@gmail.com

Smile Equestrian (Area 17)
Marian Tennyson, 30A Tullygarden Road, Armagh, County Armagh, BT61 8QT.
07776 394887
mariantennyson@hotmail.co.uk

SMS Equestrian (Area 14)
Sarah Mitchell Sheppard, The Stables, Green Drove, Fovant, Salibury, Wilts, SP3 5JG.
07843 603147
smsbookings@outlook.com

Smugglers Equestrian Centre (Area 10)
Amber Pryce, Pen-Deri Farm Lane, Manmoel, Blackwood, Caerphilly, NP12 0HU.
01495 226658
melissa@smugglers-ec.co.uk

Snowdon Farm Riding School (Area 6)
Emily McManus, Snowdon Lane, Troway, Sheffield, South Yorkshire, S21 5RT.
01246 417172
cath.meehan@btconnect.com

Somerby Equestrian Centre (Area 6)
Gail Stimson, Newbold Lane, Somerby,
Leicestershire, LE14 2PP.
01664 454838
somerbyequestriancentre@hotmail.com

South Farm Riding Stables (Area 11)
Christine Ball, Eagle Cottage, South Farm,
Langton Green, Tunbridge Wells, TN3 9JN.
01892 864401
june.southfarm17@uwclub.net

Southborough Lane Stables (Area 11)
Victoria Jackson, 321A Southborough Lane,
Bromley, Kent, BR2 8BG.
0208 467 5236
jumpinggeegees@hotmail.com

Southview Equestrian Centre (Area 6)
Rachel Baker, London Road, Silk Willoughby,
Lincolnshire, NG34 8RU.
01529 455676 - 07718 751405
rachel87emma@gmail.com

Springbank Riding School (Area 5)
ALisha Lamb, Spring Bank, Willymoor Lane,
Tushingham, Whitchurch, SY13 4QW.
07984 524573
sbridingschool@aol.com

Squirrells Riding School (Area 11)
Hayley Squirell, 116 Common Road,
Blue Bell Hill, Kent, ME5 9RG.
01634 681000
i.squirrell@sky.com

St Leonards Equitation Centre (Area 16)
Kathryn Reeve, Polston, Launceston, Cornwall,
PL15 9QR.
01566 775543
info@stleonardsequestrian.co.uk

St Patricks Way Stables (Area 17)
Sharon Madine, Mearne Road, Downpatrick,
BT30 6SY.
07414 922528
stpatrickswaystables@hotmail.co.uk

Stag Lodge (Area 11)
Melanie Gatt, Stag Lodge Stables, 197 Robin
Hood Way, London, SW20 0AA.
0208 949 6999
info@staglodgestables.com

Standing Stone Stables (Area 16)
Natalie Stevens, Standing Stone Stables,
Lelant, St. Ives, Cornwall, TR26 3HE.

Stanley Brae Pony Club at Crookgate Riding School (Area 2)
Kellie Davidson, Stanley Brae Ridng School,
Crookgate, Newcastle upon Tyne, NE16 6NS.

Stepney Bank Stables (Area 2)
Sarah Newson, Stepney Bank Stables,
Stepney Bank, Newcastle upon Tyne,
Tyne and Wear, NE1 2NP.
0191 261 5544
sara.newson@stepneybankstables.com

Stickney Riding Centre (Area 6)
Sharon Poole, Highfield House, Main Road,
Stickney, Boston, PE22 8AG.
07716 106325
stickneyridingcentre@gmail.com

Stoke Lane Stables (Area 14)
Kate Kirkpatrick, Stoke Lane Stables,
Stoke Lane, Wincanton, Somerset, BA9 9NY.
01963 32638 / 07843047277
stokelanestables@gmail.com

Stonar School Equestrian Centre (Area 14)
Stonar School, Atworth, Melksham, Wiltshire,
SN12 8NT.

01225 701766
ridingoffice@stonarschool.com

Stourport Riding Centre (Area 7)
Gemma Ash, Hartlebury Road, Stourport, Worcestershire, DY13 9JD.
01299 251125
enquiries@stourportridingcentre.co.uk

Summerfield Stables (Area 7)
Kirsty Froggatt, Brookwood Avenue, Hall Green, Birmingham, B28 0DA,
07380533118
summerfieldstables96@gmail.com

Sunnybank Equestrian Centre (Area 10)
Terina Pesci-Griffiths, Rudry Road, Rudry, Caerphilly, CF83 3DT.
07767 374079
terinna@sunnybankec.com

Talygarn Equestrian Centre (Area 10)
Amelia Rogers, Talygarn, Pontyclun, Rhondda Cynon Taff, Glamorgan, CF72 9JT.
01443 225107
talygarn@googlemail.com

Tandridge Priory Riding Centre (Area 11)
Sophie Whelan, Barrow Green Road, Oxted, Surrey, RH8 9NE.
01883 712863
tandridgeprioryridingcentre@gmail.com

Tedworth Equestrian (Area 14)
Pip Lake, Humber Lane, Tidworth, Wiltshire, SP9 7AW.
01980 846464
office@tedworthequestrian.com

Tewkesbury Pony Club Centre (Area 9)
Jo Bowen, Cherry Orchard Lane, Twyning, Tewkesbury, Gloucestershire, GL20 6JH.
07879 027790
info@hillviewlakes.biz

The 4 Gaits Riding School (Area 11)
Lisa Evans, Bislington Priory Equestrian Centre, Priory Road, Ashford, TN25 7AU,
07706 039360
lisaevans307@gmail.com

The British Racing School (Area 8)
Zoe Hammond, The British Racing School, Snailwell Road, Newmarket, Cambridgeshire, CB8 7NU.
01638 665103
Jackie.gill@brs.org.uk

The Daimler Foundation (Area 19)
Christopher McGiff, Meikle Mosside Farm Cottage, Kilmarnock, East Ayrshire, KA3 6AY.
01560600169
enquiries@thedaimlerfoundation.co.uk

The Elms (Area 9)
Sarah Hance, Equestrian Centre, The Elms School, Colwall, Malvern, Worcestershire, WR13 6EF.
Sarah.Hance@elmsschool.co.uk

The Leys Riding School (Area 1)
Haylie Lawson, Leys of Boysack Farm, Leys Mill Arbroath, DD11 4RT.
07813989088
haylielawson@hotmail.co.uk

The Oaklands School of Riding (Area 6)
Lottie Price, 174 Thrussington Road, Ratcliffe on the Wreake, Leicester, Leicestershire, LE7 4SQ.
01162 387570
lotty_1995123@hotmail.com

The Owl House Stables (Area 11)
Rachel Wright, The Owl House, Station Road, Dover, Kent, CT15 6HN.
01304 852035
owlstables@aol.com

The Ramblers Pony Club (Area 8)
Nicola Birch, The Ramblers, Silverbirch Farm, Leigh-on-Sea, Essex, SS9 5DE.
0734454858
theramblersridingclub@gmail.com

The Stables at Cissbury (Area 11)
Rebecca Brownrigg, Nepcote, Findon, West Sussex, BN14 0SR.
01903 872747
thestables@cissbury.com

The Talland School of Equitation (Area 9)
Emma Harford, Dairy Farm, Cirencester, Gloucestershire, GL7 5FD.
01285 740155
secretary@talland.net

Thompson House Equestrian Centre (Area 4)
Hana Raynes, Off Pepper Lane, Wigan, Greater Manchester, WN6 0PP.
01942 233422
hr@my-life.org.uk

Throstle Nest Riding School (Area 3)
Jeannette Wheeler, Laneside, Wilsden, Yorkshire, BD15 0LQ.
07501 257978
wilsdenequestriancentre@gmail.com

Timbertops Equestrian Centre (Area 11)
Jasmine Forsdick, Timbertops Farm, Old Maidstone Road, Sidcup, Kent, DA14 5AR.
02083 008506
jasmine.ellis@hotmail.co.uk

Tipton Hall Riding School (Area 9)
Sue Benbow, Cherry Fields, Tedstone, Delamere, Bromyard, Herefordshire, HR7 4PR.
07792358742
sue@tiptonhall.co.uk

Tong Lane End Equestrian Centre (Area 3)
Pamela Crosby, Westgate Hill Street, Bradford, Yorkshire, BD4 0SB.
01274 686332 - 07714150103
tleequestriancentre@hotmail.co.uk

Trent Park Equestrian Centre (Area 8)
Val Borrow, East Pole Farmhouse, Bramley Road, London, N14 4UW.
02083 638630
ponyclub@trentpark.com

Tullymurray Equestrian Centre (Area 17)
Sarah Turley, 145 Ballyduggan Road, Downpatrick, Co Down, BT30 8HH.
02844 811880
sarahjgething@aol.com

Tumpy Green Equestrian & Competition Centre (Area 9)
Kelly Lessel, Tumpy Green Lane, Cam, Dursley, Gloucestershire, GL11 5HZ.
01453 899002
tumpygreenequestriancentre@gmail.com

Underhill Riding Stables (Area 10)
Jessica Bufton, Dolau, Llandrindod Wells, Powys, LD1 5TL.
01597 851890
info@underhillridingstables.co.uk

Valley Farm Equestrian Centre Ltd (Area 7)
Stephanie Faulkner, Mollington Lane, Shotteswell, Banbury, Oxfordshire, OX17 1HZ.
01295 730576 / 07852
denisefaulkneruk@aol.com

Vaux Park Polo (Area 15)
Tim Vaux,
07703524613
vppc@btinternet.com

Wardhaugh Farm (Area 1)
Julie Thompson, Inverkeithny, Huntly, Aberdeenshire, AB54 7XE.
01466 781803
wardhaughfarm@gmail.com

Wardhouse Equestrian Centre (Area 19)
Louise McQuilkie, Forehouse Road, Kilbarchan, Renfrewshire, PA10 2PU.
01505 702565
wardhouse.equestrian@gmail.com

Waterstock Dressage Ltd (Area 12)
Sophie Brown, Waterstock Pony Club, Waterstock, Oxfordshire, OX33 1JS.
07711276996
arabella@waterstockdressage.com

Wellgrove Farm Equestrian (Area 11)
Emma-Kate Whittaker, Wellgrove Oast, Kings Toll Road, Pembury, Kent, TN2 4BE.
01892 822087
enquiries@wellgrovestables.co.uk

Wellington Riding (Area 13)
Allye Cutler, Basingstoke Road, Heckfield, Hook, Hampshire, RG27 0LJ.
01189 326308
ridinginfo@wellington.co.uk

Wellsfield Equestrian Centre (Area 19)
Clayton Harris, Stirling Road, Denny, Stirlingshire, FK6 6QZ.
01324 820022
enquiries@wellsfield.co.uk

Whiteleaf Riding Stables (Area 11)
Whiteleaf Stables, Lower Road, Sittingbourne, Kent, ME9 9LR.
01795 522512
whiteleafstables@hotmail.co.uk

Wick Riding School (Area 14)
Sam Pepperall, Wick House, Wick St Lawrence, Weston Super Mare, BS22 7YJ.
01934 515811
samatwick@aol.com

Wickstead Farm Equestrian Centre (Area 9)
Jo Stride, Eastrop, Highworth, Swindon, Wiltshire, SN6 7PP.
01793 762265
info@wicksteadfarm.co.uk

Widmer Equestrian (Area 12)
Jenny Davies, Widmer Farm, Pink Road, Lacey Green, Buckinghamshire, HP27 0PG.
01844 275139
widmerec@hotmail.co.uk

Wildwoods Riding Centre (Area 11)
Hayley Punder, Wildwoods, Motts Hill Lane, Tadworth, Surrey, KT20 5BH.
01737 812146
reception@wildwoodsriding.co.uk

Willerby Hill Riding School (Area 3)
Natasha Leak, Squirrel Lodge, Beverley Road, Hull, East Riding of Yorkshire, HU10 6NT.
07930863871
willerbyhillec@gmail.com

Willow Farm Riding School (Area 8)
Jane Russell, 20 Yarmouth Road, Ormesby St Margaret, Great Yarmouth, Norfolk, NR29 3QE.
07802 607064
m10jor@yahoo.co.uk

Wirral Riding Centre (Area 5)
Debbie McCone, Haddon Lane, Ness, Cheshire, CH64 8TA.

0151 336 3638
phil@wirralridingcentre.com

Witham Villa Riding Centre (Area 7)
Hannah Heaslip, Cosby Road,
Broughton Astley, Leicestershire, LE9 6PA.
01455 282694
withamvillarc@yahoo.co.uk

Witherslack Hall Equestrian Centre (Area 4)
Deana Tarr, Witherslack Hall Farm,
Witherslack, Grange-Over-Sands, Cumbria,
LA11 6SD.
01539 552244
info@whec.co.uk

Woodbine Stables (Area 7)
Cjay Jarvis, Woodbine Farm,
Grandborough Fields, Nr Rugby,
Warwickshire, CV23 8BA.
07908 975164
sue@woodbine-stables.co.uk

Worcester Riding School and Pony Club Centre (Area 9)
Deni Harper-Adams, Lower Clifton Farm,
Clifton, Severn Stoke, Worcestershire, WR8 9JF.
07889 569009
denihal@icloud.com

Wrea Green Equitation Centre (Area 4)
Amy Nunn, Bryning Lane, Bryning,
Wrea Green, Nr Kirkham, Lancashire, PR4 3PP.
01772 686576
anunn0785@gmail.com

PONY CLUB INTERNATIONAL ALLIANCE

AUSTRALIA

ponyclubaustralia.com.au

CEO Matt Helmers
ceo@ponyclubaustralia.com.au

Chair Heather Disher
chair@ponyclubaustralia.com.au

National Office info@ponyclubaustralia.com

CANADA

canadianponyclub.org

Chairman Namoi Girling
national_chair@canadianponyclub.org
janegoodliffe@gmail.com

Admin Annette Buis
info@canadianponyclub.org

HONG KONG

hongkongponyclub.com

DC dc@hongkongponyclub.com

Sec secretary@hongkongponyclub.com

NEW ZEALAND

nzpca.org

Chair Emma Barker
nzemmabarker@icould.com

CEO Lizette Turnbull
chiefexec@nzpca.org

Admin Michelle Single
admin@nzpca.org

REPUBLIC OF IRELAND

irishponyclub.ie

Chairman Michael Essame
chairman@irishponyclub.ie

CEO Sharon Monahan
ceo@irishponyclub.ie

Office office@irishponyclub.ie

SOUTH AFRICA

ponyclubsa.org.za

Chairman Cecile Watt
cecilewatt@mweb.co.za

Office nationalinfo@ponyclubsa.org.za

UNITED STATES OF AMERICA

ponyclub.org

President Jennifer Sweet
jennifers@ponyclub.org

Exec Director Teresa Woods
executivedirector@ponyclub.org

Office Admin Mary Beaven
officeadmin@ponyclub.org

EURO PONY CLUB

AUSTRIA
Gillian Schorn
gill.schorn@gps@aon.at

BELGIUM
Anne Depiesse
secretariat@ffe.be

FRANCE
Tania Melikian
tania.melikian@ffe.com

GERMANY
Maria Schierhoelter-Otte

HUNGARY
Eszter Kovacs (Secretary & Board Member)
keszter@poniklub.hu

IRELAND
Sylvaine Galligan (Treasurer & Board Member)
sylvainegalligan@gmail.com

ITALY
Mrs Christofolettis
info@scuderiadellacapinera.it
alexvirgolici@yahoo.com

LEBANON
Carla Katouah
ck@equisystem.info

NETHERLANDS
Marinus Vos
mjvos@freeler.nl

POLAND
Antony Chlapowski
info@centrumhipiki.com

ROMANIA
Vadim Virgolici (Vice-President & Board Member)
mschierhoelter@fn-dokr.de

SPAIN
Rafael Villalòn Gòmez
rafa@escuelahipicalaespuela.es

SWEDEN
Margareta Wetterberg (President & Board Member)
margareta.wetterburg@telia.com

TURKEY
Tulya Kurtulan
tulya@t-ask.org.tr

UK
Angela Yeoman (Board Member)
ayeoman@btinternet.com

OVERSEAS PONY CLUB CENTRES

OVERSEAS CENTRE COORDINATOR

overseas.centres@pcuk.org

AUSTRIA

Reit und Fahrstall Romerhutte

Nina Lauri, Reigl 11, Sankt Lorenzen am Weschel, 8242, Austria
reitstallroemerhuette@gmx.at www.
reitverein-römerhütte.at

BAHRAIN

Twin Palms Riding Centre

Abigail Peck, Twin Palms Riding Centre, RD2542, Block 252, Saar, Bahrain, RD2542
ponyclub@twinpalmsridingcentre.com

CAYMAN ISLANDS

Cayman Riding School

Tracey Rose, Cayman Riding School, Hirst Road, Savannah Newlands, Grand Cayman
caymanridingschool@gmail.com
caymanridingschool.business.site

Equestrian Centre of the Cayman Islands

Mary Alberga, Equestrian Centre of the Cayman Islands, PO Box 818, Grand Cayman, KY1 1103
equestriancentercayman@gmail.com

CHINA

Equuleus International Riding Club

Equuleus International Riding Club, No. 91, Shun Bai Road, Cuigezhuang County, Chao Yang District, Beijing, China, 100102
ponyclub@equriding.com
equriding.com

JAMAICA

Caymanas Pony Club

Heidi Lalor, Caymanas Pony Club, Caymanas Estate,
Kingston, Jamaica
hlalor@icwi.com
caymanasponyclub.com

MALAYSIA

Kuala Lumpur Pony Club Linked Centre

The Royal Selangor Polo Club, No. 1 Lorong Kelab Polo Di Raja, Kuala Lumpur 55000
Peter Abisheganaden
ztpete84@gmail.com
KLacademyofpolo.com

SINGAPORE

Bukit Timah Saddle Club

Bukit Timah Saddle Club, 51 Fairways Drive, Singapore, 286965
ponyclub@btsc.org.sg
btsc.org.sg

SUDAN

Khartoum International Community School

Khartoum International Community School, PO Box 1840, Khartoum, Sudan
kics.sd

SAUDI ARABIA

Riyadh Stables O/S

Al Jenadriyah, Riyadh Saudi Arabia
riyadhstables@gmail.com

SWITZERLAND

Bonnie Ponies

Pia Stettler, Bonnie Ponies, Hinterauli 4, CH-8492 Wila
contact@bonnieponies.ch
bonnieponies.ch

UNITED ARAB EMIRATES

Al Habtoor Polo Resort and Club

Al Habtoor Polo Resort and Club, Al Habtoor Riding School, Dubai Land, Behind the Villa, Dubai, UAE, PO Box 32304
ridingschool@alhabtoorpoloclub.com

Al Marmoom Equestrian Club

Yana Shuhaylo, Al-Marmoom Equine Therapy, Al Qudra Road, Al Marmoom Area, Dubai, UAE, PO Box 939788
info@marmoom.net
marmoom.net

Desert Palm Riding Centre

Desert Palm Riding Centre, PO Box 103635
Dubai, UAE
ridingschool@desertpalmllc.com

Dubai Polo and Equestrian Club

Dubai Polo and Equestrian Club, P.O. Box 7477,
Arabian Ranches
Dubai , United Arab Emirates
abigailb@poloclubdubai.com

Sharjah Equestrian & Racing Club

Annie Haresign, Al Qudra Road, Opposite Arabian Ranches next to Studio City, United Arab Emirates
aharesign@yahoo.co.uk
serc.ae

UNITED STATES OF AMERICA

Stargazey's Equine Therapy

1322 Country Club Rd, Jackson, Ohio OH,
45640 hread@stargazeysequinetherapy.com
stargazeysequinetherapy.com/

INDEX

Printed in Great Britain
by Amazon

46522998R00077